The Book of
CUTTINGS for
ACTING and DIRECTING

Marshall Cassady

National Textbook Company
NTC a division of NTC *Publishing Group* • Lincolnwood, Illinois USA

8 9 0 VP 9 8 7 6 5 4 3 2 1

To Mary Maloy and Tom Elrod,
and in memory of Dr. Bedrord Thurman

Acknowledgments

Antigone by Sophocles. Reprinted from *The Oedipus Cycle: An English Version* by Dudley Fitts and Robert Fitzgerald. Copyright © 1939 by Harcourt Brace Jovanovich, Inc., renewed 1967 by Dudley Fitts and Robert Fitzgerald. Reprinted by permission of the publisher.

Blood Wedding by Federico García Lorca. Reprinted from *Three Tragedies*. Copyright 1947, 1955 by New Directions Publishing Corporation.

Blue Earth by Arthur Winfield Knight. Copyright 1988 by Arthur Winfield Knight. Reprinted by permission of the author and *Crazyquilt*.

Death of a Salesman by Arthur Miller. Copyright 1949, renewed © 1977 by Arthur Miller. All rights reserved. Reprinted by permission of Viking-Penguin, Inc.

The Effect of Gamma Rays on Man-in-the-Moon Marigolds by Paul Zindel. Copyright © 1971 by Paul Zindel. CAUTION: Professionals and amateurs are hereby warned that *The Effect of Gamma Rays on Man-in-the-Moon Marigolds,* being fully protected under the copyright laws of the United States of America, the British Commonwealth, including the Dominion of Canada, and all other countries of the Berne and Universal Copyright Conventions, is subject to royalty. All rights, including professional, amateur, motion picture, recitation, lecturing, public reading, radio and television broadcasting, and the rights of translation into foreign languages, are strictly reserved. Particular emphasis is laid on the question of readings, permission for which must be secured in writing from the author's agent, Peter Hagen, William Morris Agency, 1350 Ave. of the Americas, New York, NY 10019. The amateur acting rights of *The Effect of Gamma Rays on Man-in-the-Moon Marigolds* are controlled exclusively by the Dramatists' Play Service, 440 Park Ave. S., New York, NY 10016. For excerpts and other print rights in English, contact the Junior Books Per-

CONTENTS

Introduction

In *The Book of Cuttings for Acting and Directing,* drama students can find a wide range of material. Even though the discussion questions emphasize concerns of directing, the cuttings include a selection of roles for the acting student. The book can be used exclusively by either student actors or directors. Ideally, it will be used simultaneously to give training to both.

The excerpted plays range from ancient Greek drama to the very modern, encompassing a variety of historical periods and styles. Also included are a number of genres, from Elizabethan comedy to modern tragedy, as well as many character types. When acting and directing students use the book concurrently, analysis of the cuttings should be a cooperative effort. Such cooperation, with many artists working toward a common goal, is one of the most exciting aspects of theatre.

Although students using *The Book of Cuttings* may wish to establish atmosphere and character through simple costuming and make-up, this is not essential. Neither is it necessary nor even practical to have elaborate settings, since the length of the cuttings allows for two or more to be presented during a single class period. But it may help in the interpretation of the play to have a setting in mind.

The discussion in "Preparing the Cuttings" will suggest those areas to be considered in planning the presentations. These are merely guidelines which can be elaborated on. However, students do need to keep in mind the ideas presented in this section, paying particular attention to the analysis sheets, which can perhaps be retyped and duplicated for each presentation.

Introductions to the cuttings provide the time, the setting, and the general background needed to understand the action. The cuttings have been chosen so that they can stand alone. Although they may leave the larger problems or conflicts of the play unsolved, in themselves they do make sense. The discussion questions following each cutting will help in interpreting and presenting the action. They should be considered before the cuttings are presented. In a few instances, a character will have only one line in a cutting. If desired, these lines and characters can be cut.

Remember that any number of interpretations can prove workable for each cutting. Part of the magic of theatre is that no actor or director will interpret a role, a scene, or a play in exactly the same way. Yet each person can learn from the others.

The cuttings are intended only for use in expanding knowledge of acting and directing. They are not intended for polished performance before an audience. Good luck!

PREPARING THE CUTTINGS

The cuttings have been chosen to give you a chance to interpret and then act in or direct a wide variety of plays from many historical periods. Before presenting them, you should try to read the entire play from which they are taken. That way you will gain a better idea of how the cuttings fit into the overall action. You also will see how the characters fit into the play as a whole, what their relationships with each other are, and what facets of their personalities are not revealed in the excerpted material.

After you've read through the cuttings, use the questions and forms at the end of this section for your analysis. Once you determine the direction of the action and interpret the characters, you can begin to see how everything fits together to provide a unified whole.

Two Gentlemen of Verona
Photo by Bill Reid
Courtesy of Old Globe Theatre,
San Diego, California

1

The Director

The director is usually the first theatre artist involved in bringing a script to life before an audience. A director's duties begin long before the first rehearsal is called. Much of the director's work involves analyzing the script and interpreting the play.

After deciding on the overall concept to be used, the director then meets with the set and lighting designers, the costumers, and possibly the makeup artist.

Many directors like to work out their interpretation of the script in detail before meeting with the designers or actors. Others plan the production only after these meetings.

Next, the director holds auditions, casts the play, approves the basic designs, and works with the actors. The director is responsible for the total production and has the final say in all of its aspects.

Once the play is cast, rehearsals begin with read-throughs and discussion, after which the director *blocks* the play. This means telling the actors where and how to move. Finally, the director sees that all the elements of the production fit together as a unified whole.

The Actor's Job

Directors deal with the overall interpretation and analysis of characters and their relationships, but they leave the subtleties to the actors. Although the director is responsible for the total production, the actor is more directly responsible for interpreting a specific character and determining how this character will be portrayed.

Of course, the director has to agree with the interpretation. For example, an actor might decide that the character requires a broad acting style, whereas the director envisions a more subtle portrayal. If the director insists, the actor will have to adapt to this. Yet most good productions involve compromise and a willingness to try to see the other person's point of view.

Generally, actors determine much more specifically what their characters are like. It is up to them to fill out their roles, to make the characters believable within the framework of the play.

Actors need to fill in the details of a character's background, adding to the clues given in the script. No character is complete. But by examining the "given circumstances," the actor can build a logical character, consistent in all respects with the information provided by the playwright.

Some directors give the actors a great deal of latitude in interpreting character. Others work out every element of the production in great detail.

Specifics of Directing

A play in script form is not a finished work. It needs the addition of the director, the designers, the actors, and the audience to bring it to life.

Although all directors approach their jobs differently, one of the first considerations is determining the play's theme or central idea, the playwright's purpose, so it can be emphasized through such devices as proper line delivery and placement on the stage.

To determine the central idea, it helps to be familiar with the playwright's life, which often helps explain why a playwright wrote as he or she did. Sometimes knowing the historical period can help explain why someone wrote in a certain way.

After deciding on the overall interpretation, directors then become more specific in their analysis. An important aspect is figuring out where the major climax and minor climaxes occur, so that both can be appropriately emphasized.

The director first determines the prevailing mood or atmosphere. Is it comic, tragic, nostalgic, or perhaps inspirational? How can this mood be maintained?

Next, the director moves on to the characters. How do they fit into the play as a whole? Why are they included? What is their specific purpose in advancing the plot? In determining these things, the director figures out the characters' basic traits and how they relate to each other. The director determines how each character advances the theme and symbolizes a basic human need or want, and how these needs and wants come into conflict.

The director then may work on determining what type of environment will effectively portray the atmosphere, mood, actions, and circumstances of the characters. What elements of the design are necessary? Should the setting be realistic, fragmentary, or completely nonrealistic? What style best suits the action?

After this the director plans the blocking, using a prompt book. This is the script set in the middle of a larger page to allow margins for notes. Directors keep records of the blocking in two ways.

The first is simply by writing out where each actor is and when and where he or she should move. (During the blocking rehearsals the actors should always carry pencils to write in their own movement.) Another is to use tiny drawings of the set, including set pieces. For interior scenes, this would consist of furniture and appliances; for exterior scenes, it would include rocks, trees, and small buildings. Then through the use of lines and arrows, the director makes a sketch indicating when and where the actors should move. These drawings appear in the margins beside the lines on or after which the actors move. Because what looked good on paper does not always work on the stage, the blocking often is changed, and records generally are kept using a pencil rather than a pen. A sample prompt book page can be seen in Figure 1.

Finally, the rehearsals begin. There are six types. First are *reading rehearsals,* which usually take place in an informal atmosphere, with little emphasis on correct line interpretation. They allow the actors to become used to each other, to the director, and to the script. During the reading rehearsals the director explains his or her interpretation of the play and discusses the technical aspects of the production. The actors may be shown sketches of the set, costumes, and lighting.

Next are the *blocking rehearsals,* in which the actors are given their directions. Then come *character and line rehearsals,* in which the actors continue to build their characters and polish the delivery of lines. These are followed by *finishing rehearsals,* in which all the elements of acting are developed and unified. The last two types of rehearsals are *technical rehearsals,* in which the elements of setting, light, sound, and properties are coordinated with the action, and *dress rehearsals,* which are presented in full costume and makeup, exactly as if they were finished performances.

Figure 1. Sample prompt book page.

COLONEL: And you fell into the abyss of Catholicism.

BENEDICTA: Colonel, you have a distinct gift for shading a statement of fact to make it fit your own conclusions.

COLONEL: An old trick of my trade, Sister. Never allow the enemy the indulgence of accepting a positive statement.

[handwritten: colonel turns toward her. she crosses to sofa]

BENEDICTA: Am I your enemy, Colonel?

COLONEL: I don't know, Sister. I hope to find out.

BENEDICTA: Then I am guilty until proven innocent?

[handwritten: she sits]

COLONEL: Guilty? of what, Sister?

[handwritten: He smiles—mocking her and crosses to the downstage arm of the chair and sits.]

BENEDICTA: I don't know, Colonel, I hope to find out.

(*They both laugh.*)

COLONEL: Very good, Sister. You've won the point, but I've won my bet.

BENEDICTA: Bet, Colonel?

COLONEL: Yes. You know Field Major Wollman, your military governor?

BENEDICTA: Only by sight. He has been here visiting.

[handwritten: she crosses upstage, rearranges flowers in a vase on the small table]

COLONEL: Well, he knows you. When he found I was coming here, he said "Watch that Benedicta, the brooding one, she never smiles."

BENEDICTA: He wasn't very gallant.

[handwritten: she crosses to the sofa and sits]

COLONEL: I defended you, Sister. I defended womankind. I said there wasn't a woman alive who never smiles. So we bet on it.

[handwritten: He rises, crosses behind her and stands over her]

BENEDICTA: And you won.

[handwritten: He keeps tapping his riding crop against the heel of his boot.]

6

THE STAGE

It is important to present a pleasing picture to the audience at all times during a play. This means the stage should be balanced. Unless there is a good reason, actors rarely turn their backs on the audience in a picture-frame theater. (Of course, they would have to in theatre-in-the-round.) The director and actors need to be aware of sightlines, so that each actor is visible to any member of the audience at any moment. This is the reason that the outer walls of a setting often are angled inward.

Movement and business should be motivated by the script or should help portray character.

There are two types of business, inherent and supplementary. The first advances the story or is important to the plot. It includes such things as exits, entrances, and phone calls, everything that is called for in the script. Supplementary business is added for effect, either to establish character or to emphasize the play's central idea. It includes how a character stands, sits, and walks. It helps establish the mood of the scene and the emotions of the character.

Both types of business are used for emphasis. A moving actor demands more attention than one who is stationary. Focus or emphasis also can be provided by having the important character positioned higher than the others, that is, standing while the others sit or on a platform while the others remain on floor level. Emphasis can be provided by having one actor stand apart from the group, or by placing the important character upstage and having the others look in that direction.

Strength is established when a character moves directly from one point to another. Wandering or random movement suggests weakness. A strong character generally moves in front of furniture rather than behind it.

Some areas of the stage are stronger than others. Downstage center is the strongest, with the upstage corners, those nearest the back wall, the weakest. Of course, this can be counterbalanced by having the other actors focus their attention toward the back or by having the upstage character on a high platform.

Analyzing the Cuttings

F ollowing are two forms, one for actors to use in determining their characters, the other for directors. You may wish to photocopy the forms on pages 12 through 15 and use them to analyze each character or play you study. The forms are preceded by questions that may help in determining interpretation. First are general questions to be answered by both actors and directors; these are followed by specific questions for actors or directors.

The Play as a Whole

1. What do you know about the playwright? When and where did he or she live? Did environment and background affect what the person wrote? What affected the writing most?

2. What is the play about? What is the central idea? How does it affect the progression of the action and the type of characters that are included?

3. How is the play structured? Where are the high and low points? Is it comic or tragic? This will help determine how the character is portrayed. For example, comedy usually has a broader or more exaggerated style than does tragedy.

4. What are the circumstances of time and place? Where does the action occur? How is this similar to or different from the world in which we live? Are there special social or economic conditions that affect the characters?

The Cutting

1. Where are the high points of the action and what are the most important lines? Figuring this out can help in planning blocking that emphasizes ideas and speeches.

2. How do the characters interact? What kinds of relationships do they have? What are their psychological and emotional ties?

The Actor's Analysis

1. What is the character's background? What kind of education does he or she have? What sort of family does he or she come from? Where did the character grow up and later live? What has played the biggest part in shaping the character's personality?

2. What are the character's interests? What kind of work does the character do or want to do? Why? How does he or she like to spend free time? If the character has a house or apartment, how is it furnished? Why?

3. What character traits are evident? How does the character impress other people? Is he or she generally happy or unhappy? What are the most important aspects of his or her personality? What are the dominant traits? What kinds of friends does she or he have?

4. How does the character feel about others? About self? About the world in general?

On the basis of the answers, figure out how to portray the character from manner of speaking to type of walk and movement. Try to justify what you've decided on the basis of the background you've determined.

Do not be limited only by the questions above. Try to think of any others that might help present a complete picture of the character in order to make the person come across as real or believable.

Two Gentlemen of Verona
Photo by Bill Reid
Courtesy of Old Globe Theatre, San Diego, California

The Director's Analysis

1. What are the characters' basic traits? How are the characters related? How do they feel about each other? What in their personalities provides the conflict between them? Who is the most important character in each scene? Why? How can this be pointed up? How is each character unique? How is each stereotypical?

2. Which are the most important lines in this scene? Which are important in establishing character? In advancing the plot? How can these lines be pointed up for the audience?

3. What is the subject matter of the play? Why is this important? Why would an audience want to see this play with this subject matter? How can you convey the play's importance to an audience?

4. What is the atmosphere of the play? What type of setting would best portray this? What type of setting, lighting, costuming, and makeup would be appropriate for the play? Why?

Actor's Analysis

Play ————————————————————————

Playwright ————————————————————

Cutting ——————————————————————

My Character ————————————————————

My Character's Background:

    A. Social

    B. Educational

    C. Geographic

    D. Family

    E. Major Influences

    F. Environment (Time and Place)

Interests

    A. Jobs

B. Hobbies

C. Friends

D. Other Activities

Personality Traits:

Relationship with Other Characters:

Goals:

Playwright's Life and Influences on Writing the Play:

Theme and Meaning of the Play:

Brief Description of the Other Characters:

Director's Analysis

Play ———————————————————————

Playwright ———————————————————————

Cutting ———————————————————————

Theme or Central Idea:

Metaphor:

Character Descriptions:

    A. Character 1

    B. Character 2

    C. Character 3

    D. Character 4

    E. Character 5

The Goals of Each Character:

Why Each Character Is Included:

How Each Character Advances the Cutting:

The Basic Struggle or Conflict of the Cutting:

The Needs of Each Character:

Diagram of the set, showing placement of set pieces, such as furniture, trees, rocks, and so on.

MONOLOGUES FOR MEN

In White America

Ties

Hamlet, Prince of Denmark

Hamlet
Photo courtesy of Kent State
University Theatre, Kent, Ohio

Act 1

In White America

Martin B. Duberman

Through the use of recorded history, including letters, diaries, and newspaper accounts, the play documents the history of blacks in the United States. Since there are no continuing characters throughout, the actors usually portray a number of different people, switching quickly from one to the other. In the original production, three black actors and three white actors played all the roles.

According to a note at the front of the acting edition, the play should be presented as simply as possible with a minimum of properties. Of course, there can be no elaborate set because the scenes switch from location to location and from one time period to another.

JOURDON ANDERSON: To My Old Master, Colonel P. H. Anderson, Big Spring, Tennessee.

Sir: I got your letter, and was glad to find that you had not forgotten Jourdon, and that you wanted me to come back and live with you again. Although you shot at me twice before I left you, I am glad you are still living.

I want to know particularly what the good chance is you propose to give me. I am doing tolerably well here. I get twenty-five dollars a month, with victuals and clothing; have a comfortable home for Mandy,—the folks call her Mrs. Anderson,—and the children—Milly, Jane and Grundy—go to school and are learning well. The teacher says Grundy has a head for a preacher. They go to Sunday school, and Mandy and me attend church regularly. We are kindly treated.

Mandy says she would be afraid to go back without some proof that you were disposed to treat us justly and kindly; and we have concluded to test your sincerity by asking you to send us our wages for the time we served you. This will make us forget and forgive old scores, and rely on your justice and friendship in the future. I served you faithfully for thirty-two years, and Mandy for twenty years. At twenty-five dollars a month for me, and two dollars a week for Mandy, our earnings would amount to eleven thousand six hundred and eighty dollars. Add to this the interest for the time our wages have been kept back, and deduct what you paid for our clothing, and three doctor's visits to me, and pulling a tooth for Mandy, and the balance will show what we are in justice entitled to. Please send the money by Adam's Express, in care of V. Winters, Esq., Dayton, Ohio.

Say howdy to George Carter, and thank him for taking the pistol from you when you were shooting at me.

From your old servant,
Jourdon Anderson

Interpretation

1. There is a great deal of irony in this monologue. Point out and discuss examples and determine how you as director or actor would emphasize this.

2. What sort of setting would you visualize for this cutting?

3. What can you infer about the character of Jourdon Anderson? How would you portray these traits for an audience?

4. In what ways might the actor in this cutting carry himself? Move? Speak?

5. Often in a play what is left unsaid or implied is as important or even more important than the text itself. It is called the subtext. What are some things Anderson is stating without using the actual words?

scene 1

Ties

Marsh Cassady

T he following monologue introduces the play, which is written in a series of eleven scenes and an epilogue, all dealing with the relationship between the two men and the narrator. The action covers a period of more than forty years and involves the relationship of the two characters as seen through the eyes of Boris, Melvin's son.

First presented in New York in 1986, the play details how a rather unconventional family is united against outside conflicts, despite internal tensions that at times seem ready to tear the characters apart.

At rise: [*As the audience enters the theatre, the open curtain reveals a dimly-lighted set. After everyone is seated, spotlights come up on* BORIS, *who enters DR and crosses to Center. He addresses the audience directly.*]

BORIS: Hi, my name is Boris Aradopolos. I'm the author of *Ties,* a play about humanness and love and people learning to live with one another. It's about how families are united against interference. Yet they bicker and fight with each other because they can't seem to help it. [*Pause.*] To fill you in: My mother, Lucinda, was a countess, my father a first-generation American. His name was Menolaus, although he later took the name of Melvin which he much preferred. My paternal grandparents, Nikkos and Alexandria Aradopolos, had immigrated from Greece to New England. Extremely proud of their new country, as only naturalized citizens can be, they nevertheless were determined that Dad would have the advantages of travel and a European education. He spent several years studying abroad at whatever university struck his fancy. When he was twenty-nine, a friend introduced him to my mother. Against the wishes of my maternal grandparents they married. Two days later that marriage was at an end. Possibly as some form of self-punishment, Mother stayed on at the same hotel in Leipzig where she and Dad had been honeymooning. [*Pause.*] When I was but five months old, she left me in the care of a maid at that hotel while she went across the street to have her hair done. On the way back she was struck by a car. She died instantly. [*Pause.*] My maternal grandparents wanted to have nothing to do with me. So Dad, who had never seen me before, flew to Germany to pick me up and take me home with him. Home was Southern California where he'd recently started to teach. He didn't have a Ph.D. yet, so he was at the instructor's level. That meant there was little money coming in. For the next three years a neighbor woman cared for me while he was at school. [*Pause.*] Even though Dad was sometimes too wrapped up in his work to take much time to be with me, I have wonderful memories of my childhood.

[BORIS *opens the photo album and looks at it.*]

That's why this old photo album means so much to me. Dad kept a great record of my early years and of people he thought I'd be curious about. See, here's my mother. Isn't she beautiful?

[*He holds the album so the audience sees the photos inside.*]

Here are her parents, my grandparents.

[*He shows the audience other photos as he talks.*]

And here are Grandma and Grandpa Aradopolos. He was a surgeon, and Grandma a concert pianist. But she never wanted to leave Grandpa to go on tour. Grandpa died when I was eight and Grandma two years later. She fell and broke her hip and just gave up. [*Pause.*] This is a picture of one of the times Dad and Dennis and I went on a picnic to Torrey Pines. We went all sorts of places together—to films and the zoo and art galleries. Especially to art galleries.

[BORIS *closes the album and tucks it under his arm.*]

Despite the good times we had, my clearest and sharpest early memory isn't a happy one. I was about seven, I think, and was walking home from school. A couple of older boys—they must have been ten or eleven—began taunting me about not having a mother. I tried to pretend I didn't hear them, but I told Dad about it later.

Interpretation

1. In this monologue Boris is talking about his family, not himself. Yet part of his personality is revealed. Discuss what you can discover about him.

2. What can you tell of Boris's feelings about his family and about life in general?

3. Because Boris is speaking directly to the audience, this cutting is different from most others where the actors make no acknowledgment of the spectator. How would you have Boris stand and move? Would you use any props besides the album? Why?

4. Which are the most important lines in this monologue? How, as a director, would you point them up?

5. What is the prevailing mood of the cutting? How would you convey it?

HAMLET, PRINCE of DENMARK

William Shakespeare

Hamlet is still emotionally shaken by the recent death of his father, King George. To make matters worse, his mother, Gertrude, has married his uncle, the present King Claudius, whom Hamlet hates.

This monologue, which occurs early in the play, shows his despair over the recent events. The action takes place in "a room of state in the castle."

It was customary in Shakespeare's time to let the major characters deliver monologues as a means of providing exposition, background necessary to understanding the progression of the action. Called soliloquies, they are meant to show the workings of the character's mind, much as stream-of-consciousness writing does in modern fiction.

HAMLET: Oh, that this too too solid flesh would melt,
  Thaw, and resolve itself into a dew!
  Or that the Everlasting had not fixed
  His canon[1] 'gainst self-slaughter! Oh, God! God!
  How weary, stale, flat, and unprofitable
  Seem to me all the uses[2] of this world!
  Fie on 't, ah, fie! 'Tis an unweeded garden,
  That grows to seed, things rank[3] and gross in nature
  Possess it merely.[4] That it should come to this!
  But two months dead! Nay, not so much, not two.
  So excellent a King, that was, to this,

[1]canon: rule   [2]uses: ways   [3]rank: coarse   [4]merely: entirely

Hyperion[5] to a satyr.[6] So loving to my mother
That he might not beteem[7] the winds of heaven
Visit her face too roughly. Heaven and earth!
Must I remember? Why, she would hang on him
As if increase of appetite had grown
By what it fed on. And yet within a month—
Let me not think on 't.—Frailty, thy name is woman!—
A little month, or ere those shoes were old
With which she followed my poor father's body,
Like Niobe[8] all tears.—Why she, even she—
Oh, God! A beast that wants discourse of reason[9]
Would have mourned longer—married with my uncle,
My father's brother, but no more like my father
Than I to Hercules. Within a month,
Ere yet the salt of most unrighteous tears
Had left the flushing in her gallèd[10] eyes,
She married. Oh, most wicked speed, to post[11]
With such dexterity[12] to incestuous sheets!
It is not, nor it cannot, come to good.
But break, my heart, for I must hold my tongue!

[5]Hyperion: the sun god   [6]satyr: half goat, half man   [7]beteem: allow
[8]Niobe: She boasted of her children, annoying the goddess Artemis, who
killed them. Niobe became so sorrowful that she changed into a rock,
dripping water forever.   [9]wants discourse of reason: is without ability to
reason   [10]gallèd: sore   [11]post: hurry   [12]dexterity: nimbleness

Interpretation

1. What is Hamlet's mood? Why? How would you try to convey it to
an audience?

2. What is the purpose of this soliloquy? How do you think it might
further the action of the play?

3. Using what is given in the cutting and any other information you
have about the play, describe Hamlet's character.

4. Obviously, this is a period piece. What, if anything, would you do
to convey the historical sense of the period? Why?

5. How does Hamlet feel about his father? His mother? In what way
would you convey this feeling to an audience?

6. What props or furniture would you want to use in staging the
monologue? What type of setting? Why?

MONOLOGUES FOR WOMEN

IN WHITE AMERICA

OH DAD, POOR DAD, MAMMA'S HUNG
  YOU IN THE CLOSET AND I'M FEELIN' SO
  SAD

THE TROJAN WOMEN

MISS JULIE

Oh Dad, Poor Dad
Photo by Barbara McLarney
Courtesy of Grossmont College Drama Department,
El Cajon, California

Act 1

In White America

Martin B. Duberman

There are a number of monologues in the play, all illustrative of discrimination of a sort against black people. In this monologue, Sojourner Truth, who lived in the North at the time, spoke at a Women's Rights Convention in 1851.

As the speech shows, blacks were not the only oppressed minority of the time. Black women were doubly oppressed, first because of their color and second because of their sex.

SOJOURNER TRUTH: Wall, chilern, whar dar is so much racket dar must be somethin' out o' kilter. I tink dat 'twixt de black folks of de Souf and de womin at de Norf, all talkin' 'bout rights, de white men will be in a fix pretty soon. But what's all dis here talkin' 'bout?

Dat man ober dar say dat womin needs to be helped into carriages, and lifted ober ditches, and to hab de best place everywhar. Nobody eber helps me into carriages, or ober mud-puddles, or gibs me any best place! And a'n't I a woman? Look at me! Look at my arm! I have ploughed, and planted, and gathered into barns and no man could head me! And a'n't I a woman? I have borne thirteen children, and seen 'em mos' sold off to slavery, and when I cried out with my mother's grief, none but Jesus heard me! And a'n't I a woman?

Den dey talks 'bout dis ting in de head; what dis dey call it? [*A voice whispering*]: Intellect.

Dat's it, honey. What's dat got to do wid womin's rights? If my cup won't hold but a pint, and yourn holds a quart, wouldn't ye be mean not to let me have my little half-measure full?

Den dat little man in black dar, he say women can't have as much rights as men, 'cause Christ wan't a woman! Whar did your Christ come from? Whar did your Christ come from? From God and a woman! Man had nothin' to do wid Him!

If de fust woman God ever made was strong enough to turn de world upside down all alone, dese women togedder ought to be able to turn it back, and get it right side up again! And now dey is asking to do it, de men better let 'em.

Interpretation

1. What type of person is Sojourner Truth? How can you tell that from what she says? What are her most important traits or qualities? What makes you think so?

2. What type of vocal quality would the character use? Why?

3. What props would you have Sojourner Truth use, if any? Explain.

4. What kind of stance or posture would the character use? Why?

5. Keeping in mind the need to switch scenes often in this play, what sort of setting would you want to use for this cutting?

Oh Dad, Poor Dad, Mamma's Hung You in the Closet and I'm Feelin' So Sad

Arthur Kopit

A lthough sometimes classified as part of the theatre of the absurd movement, Kopit's play differs from other absurdist drama in that the others are concerned with the absurdity of human existence in a meaningless world. Kopit, on the other hand, is saying that one should not take human existence seriously.

The play is a parody of the over-protective mother, smothering her naive, sheltered son, Jonathan. Of course, the characters are not realistic. Rather they are exaggerated to add fuel to Kopit's theme. The title comes from the fact that Madame Rosepettle, who travels extensively with Jonathan, always brings along the stuffed corpse of her husband which she hangs in the hotel room closet.

The scene that contains the following monologue opens with stage directions that state: "A clock is heard ticking softly in the distance. For an interminably long time it continues to tick while JONATHAN sits in his chair, motionless. After a while the ticking speeds up almost imperceptibly and soon after, laughter is heard. At first it is a giggle from the rear of the theatre, then a cough from the side, then a self-conscious laugh from the other side, then a full, gusty belly-roar from all corners of the theatre," and so on. This then maintains the tone established at the beginning of the play.

Madam Rosepettle has brought the Commodore to her "lavish hotel suite somewhere in the Caribbean."

MADAME ROSEPETTLE: Now you don't *really* want to leave—do you, Commodore? After all, the night is still so young—and you haven't even seen my husband yet. Besides, there's a little story I still must tell you. A bedtime story. A fairy-tale full of handsome princes and enchanted maidens; full of love and joy and music; tenderness and charm. It's my very favorite story, you see. And I never leave a place without telling it to at least one person. So please, Commodore, won't you stay? . . . *Just for a little while? [He stares at her in horror. He tries once more to push his chair back. But the chair does not move. He sinks down into it weakly. She leans across the table and tenderly touches his hand.]* Good. I knew you'd see it my way. It would have been such a shame if you'd had to leave. For you see, Commodore, we are, in a way, united. We share something in common—you and I. We share desire. For you desire me, with love in your heart. While I, my dear Commodore—desire your heart. *[She smiles sweetly and sips some more champagne.]* How simple it all is, in the end. *[She rises slowly from her chair and walks over to him. She runs her hands lovingly through his hair and down the back of his neck. The light on the table dims slightly.* MADAME ROSEPETTLE *walks slowly away. A spot of light follows her as she goes. Light on the table fades more. The* COMMODORE *sits, motionless.]* His name was Albert Edward Robinson Rosepettle III. How strange and sad he was. All the others who had come to see me had been tall, but he was short. They had been rich, while he was poor. The others had been handsome but Albert, poor Albert, he was as ugly as a humid day—*[She laughs sadly, distantly.]* and just about as wet, too. Oh, he was a fat bundle of sweat, Mr. Rose-above. He was nothing but one great torrent of perspiration. Winter and summer, spring and fall, Albert was dripping wet. Yes, he was round and wet and hideous and I never could figure out how he ever got such a name as Albert Edward Robinson Rosepettle III. Oh, I must have been very susceptible indeed to have married Albert. I *was* twenty-eight and that *is* a susceptible year in a woman's life. And of course I *was* a virgin, but still I—Oh, stop blushing, Mr. Roseabove. I'm not lying. It's all true. Part of the cause of my condition, I will admit, was due to the fact that I still hadn't gone out with a man. But I am certain, Mr. Roseabove, I am certain that despite your naughty glances my virtue would have remained unsoiled, no matter what. Oh, I had spoken to men. (Their voices are gruff.) And in crowded streets I had often brushed against them. (Their bodies, I found, are tough and bony.) I had observed their ways and habits, Mr. Roseabove. Even at that tender age I had the foresight to realize I must know what I was up against. So I watched them huddle in hallways, talking in nervous whispers and laughing when little girls passed by. I watched their hands in crowded buses and even felt their feeling elbows on crowded streets. And then, one night, when I was walking home I saw a man standing in a window. I saw him taking his contact lenses out and his hearing aid out of his ear. I saw him take his teeth out of his thin-lipped mouth and drop them into a smiling glass of water. I saw him lift his snow-white hair off his wrinkled, white head and place it on a gnarled, wooden hat tree. And then I saw him take his clothes off. And when he was done and didn't move but stood and stared at a full length mirror whose glass he had covered with towels, then I went home and wept. And so one day I bolted the door to my room. I locked myself inside, bought a small revolver just in case, then sat at my window and watched what went on below. It was not a pretty sight. Some men came up to see me. They came and knocked. I did not let them in.

"Hello in there," they said.
"Hello in there,
My name is Steven.
Steven S. (for Steven) Steven.
One is odd
But two is even.
I know you're not
So I'm not leavin'."

Or something like that [*Short pause.*] But they all soon left anyway. I think they caught the scent of a younger woman down the hall. . . . And so I listened to the constant sound of feet disappearing down the stairs. I watched a world walk by my window; a world of lechery and lies and greed. I watched a world walk by and I decided not to leave my room until this world came to me, *exactly* as I wanted it. One day Albert came toddling up the stairs. He waddled over to my room, scratched on the door and said, in a frail and very frightened voice, "Will you please marry me?" And so I did. It was as simple as that. [*Pause. Then distantly.*] I still wonder why I did it, though. I still wonder why. [*Short pause. Then, with a laugh of resignation.*] I don't really know why. I guess it just seemed like the right thing to do. Maybe it's because he was the first one who ever asked me. No, that's not right.—Perhaps it's because he was so ugly and fat; so unlike everything I'd ever heard a husband should be. No, that doesn't make much sense, either.—Perhaps it's—yet, perhaps it's because one look at Albert's round, sad face and I knew he could be mine—that no matter where he went, or whom he saw, or what he did, Albert would be mine, my husband, my lover, my own—mine to love; mine to live with:—mine to kill. [*Short pause.*] And so we were wed. That night I went to bed with a man for the first time in my life. The next morning I picked up my mattress and moved myself to another room. Not that there was something wrong with Albert. Oh, no! He was *quite* the picture of health. His pudgy, pink flesh bouncing with glee. Oh, how easily is man satisfied. How easily is his porous body saturated with "fun." All he asks is a little sex and a little food and there he is, asleep with a smile, and snoring. Never the slightest regard for you, lying in bed next to him, your eyes open wide. No, he stretches his legs and kicks you in the shins; stretches his arms and smacks you in the eye. Oh, how noble, how magical, how marvelous is love. So you see, Mr. Roseabove, I had to leave his room. For as long as I stayed there I was not safe. After all, we'd only met the day before and I knew far too little about him. But now that we were married I had time to find out more. A few of the things I wanted to know were: what had he done before we'd ever met, what had he wanted to do, what did he *still* want to do, what was he doing about it? What did he dream about while he slept? What did he think about when he stared out the window? . . . What did he think about when I wasn't near? These were the things that concerned me most. And so I began to watch him closely. My plan worked best at night, for that was when he slept—I would listen at my door until I heard his door close. Then I'd tiptoe out and watch him through his keyhole. When his lights went out I'd open up his door and creep across the floor to his bed, and then I'd listen more. My ear became a stethoscope that recorded the fluctuations of his dream life. For I was waiting for him to speak; waiting for the slightest word that might betray his sleeping, secret thoughts. . . . But, no, Albert only snored and smiled and slept on and on. And *that,* Mr. Roseabove, is how I spent my nights!—next to him; my husband, my "Love." I never left his side, never took my eyes from his sleeping face. I dare you to find me a wife who's as devoted as that. [*She laughs. Short pause.*] A month later I found that I was pregnant. It had happened that first horrible night. How like

Albert to do something like that. I fancy he knew it was going to happen all the time, too. I do believe he planned it that way. One night, one shot, one chance in a lifetime and bham! you've had it. It takes an imaginative man to miss. It takes someone like Albert to do something like that. But yet, I never let on. Oh, no. Let him think I'm simply getting fat, I said. And that's the way I did it, too. I, nonchalantly putting on weight; Albert nonchalantly watching my belly grow. If he knew what was happening to me he never let me know it. He was as silent as before. [*Pause.*] Twelve months later my son was born. He was so overdue, when he came out he was already teething. He bit the index finger off the poor doctor's hand and snapped at the nurse till she fainted. I took him home and put him in a cage in the darkest corner of my room.

Interpretation

1. Why do you think Madame Rosepettle goes on in such detail about the parts of her past discussed here? What is her objective or goal?

2. What kind of person do you think the character is? How can you tell? What is her most important trait?

3. How would Madame Rosepettle speak? Move? Carry herself? Why?

4. What is the prevailing mood of this cutting? What feelings do you want the audience viewing this to have?

THE TROJAN WOMEN

Euripides

The play takes place shortly after the capture of Troy by King Menelaus of Sparta and Agamemnon, general of the Greeks. All the Trojan men have been killed or have fled; the women and children are captives.

According to the stage directions, the scene is an open space before the city, which is visible in the background, partly demolished and smoldering.

The women have been placed in temporary housing. Kassandra's mother, Hecuba, Queen of Troy, is prostrate on the ground.

The god Poseidon announces that Priam, the King of Troy, lies unburied, that Hecuba's daughter Polyxena has been killed, and that Kassandra is to be a mistress-slave of Agamemnon.

The play is the account of the fall of Troy and the fate of its women. Even the gods themselves are appalled. Throughout, the lamentations intensify, pointing up the pathos.

The women, very much like Synge's characters in *Riders to the Sea,* are trapped within their tragic circumstances. They have been acted upon, their fate decided.

In the following monologue, the middle one of three long speeches, Kassandra appears as if in a dream wearing her bridal garlands.

Translated by Richard Lattimore

KASSANDRA: O mother, star my hair with flowers of victory.
  I know you would not have it happen thus; and yet
  this is a king I marry; then be glad; escort
  the bride. Oh, thrust her strongly on. If Loxias[1]
  is Loxias still, the Achaians' pride, great Agamemnon has won

[1]Apollo, or Phoebus.

a wife[2] more fatal than ever Helen was.
Since I will kill him; and avenge my brothers' blood
and my father's in the desolation of his house.
But I leave this in silence and sing not now the axe
to drop against my throat and other throats than mine,
the agony of the mother murdered, brought to pass
from our marriage rites, and Atreus' house made desolate.
I am ridden by God's curse still, yet I will step so far
out of my frenzy as to make plain this city's fate
as blessed beside the Achaians'. For one woman's sake,
one act of love, these hunted Helen down and threw
thousands of lives away. Their general—clever man—
in the name of a vile woman cut his darling down,
gave up for a brother the sweetness of children in his house,
all to bring back that brother's wife, a woman who went
of her free will, not caught in constraint of violence.
The Achaians came beside Skamandros' banks, and died
day after day, though none sought to wrench their land from
    them
nor their own towering cities. Those the War God caught
never saw their sons again, nor were they laid to rest
decently in winding sheets by their wives' hands, but lie
buried in alien ground; while all went wrong at home
as the widows perished, and barren couples raised and nursed
the children of others, no survivor left to tend
the tombs, and what is left there, with blood sacrificed.
For such success as this congratulate the Greeks.
No, but the shame is better left in silence, for fear
my singing voice become the voice of wretchedness.
The Trojans have that glory which is loveliest:
they died for their own country. So the bodies of all
who took the spears were carried home in loving hands,
brought, in the land of their fathers, to the embrace of earth
and buried becomingly as the rite fell due. The rest,
those Phrygians who escaped death in battle, day by day
came home to happiness the Achaians could not know;
their wives, their children. Then was Hektor's fate so sad?
You think so. Listen to the truth. He is dead and gone
surely, but with reputation, as a valiant man.
How could this be, except for the Achaians' coming?
Had they held back, none might have known how great he
    was.

[2]Helen's sister, Clytemnestra, was Agamemnon's wife. She murdered him
on his return from Troy.

The bride of Paris was the daughter of Zeus. Had he
not married her, fame in our house would sleep in silence still.
Though surely the wise man will forever shrink from war,
yet if war come, the hero's death will lay a wreath
not lustreless on the city. The coward alone brings shame.
Let no more tears fall, mother, for our land, nor for
this marriage I make; it is by marriage that I bring
to destruction those whom you and I have hated most.

Interpretation

1. What is Kassandra's mood? What in the lines tell you this?

2. The language of tragedy often is quite different from that of
comedy. How, from the lines, the flow, and the language, can you tell
this is tragedy?

3. Which lines are most important in this cutting? Why do you
think so? How would you emphasize them?

4. What do the lines tell you about Kassandra's character? What
kind of person is she?

5. Keeping in mind that there can be experimentation with setting
and costumes, such as placing historical pieces in modern dress and
so on, how would you design this play?

Miss Julie

August Strindberg

The play is written as one long act with no divisions into scenes. The title character is the daughter of a Swedish count and his strong, man-hating wife.

Julie's mother has taught her that women are superior and men are to be hated. The basic conflict of the play occurs within Julie's mind, a war between the beliefs she's been taught and her desire for a normal man-woman relationship.

Unfortunately, the man in whom she places her trust is Jean, the count's valet, who sees Julie only as a symbol of the things he wants. His goal is simply to rise above his class. To this end he sets out to seduce Julie. She succumbs to his attentions. Only later does she realize the dishonor involved and decide to commit suicide. Jean will continue to live because he lacks Julie's preoccupation with honor.

In this monologue, which takes place in the large kitchen of a Swedish manor house in the 1880s, Julie is trying to talk herself into running away with Jean, even though she knows it will not work out. She is talking to the cook, Kristin, who knows of Julie's involvement. At this point Julie is trying to fool only herself but cannot even be successful at that.

Translated by C. D. Locock

JULIE [*Presto tempo.*]: You've never been abroad, Kristin—you must have a look round the world. You can't imagine what fun it is travelling by train—new people continually—new countries—and then we'll go to Hamburg and have a look at the Zoological Gardens on our way—you'll like that—and go to the theatre and hear the opera—and when we get to Munich we shall have the picture galleries! There are Rubenses and Raphaels there—the great painters, you know.

You've heard of Munich, where King Ludwig lived—the king who went mad, you know.—And then we'll see his castle—he still has castles furnished just like they are in fairy tales—and from there it's not far to Switzerland—and the Alps! Think of the Alps covered with snow in the middle of summer—and oranges grow there, and laurels that are green all the year round. . .

[JEAN *is seen in the right wing, stropping his razor on a strop which he holds between his teeth and his left hand; he listens amused to the conversation and nods approval now and then.*]

[*Tempo prestissimo.*] And then we'll take a hotel—and I shall sit in the office while Jean stands and receives the guests . . . goes out shopping . . . writes letters.—There's life for you! Whistling trains, omnibuses driving up, bells ringing in the bedrooms and the restaurant—and I shall make out the bills— and I know how to salt them too. . . . You can't imagine how timid travellers are when it comes to paying bills! And you— you will sit in the kitchen as housekeeper in chief. Of course you won't do any cooking yourself—and you'll have to dress neatly and stylishly when you see people—and you, with your looks—no, I'm not flattering you—why, you'll be able to catch a husband one fine day! A rich Englishman, I shouldn't wonder—they're the easy ones to—[*Slackens her pace.*] catch—and then we'll get rich—and build ourselves a villa on Lake Como—of course it rains there a little occasionally— but—[*Slower.*] I suppose the sun shines sometimes—however gloomy it seems—and—then—otherwise we can come home again—and come back—[*A pause.*] here—or somewhere else—

Interpretation

1. Why is Julie talking to the cook about traveling? Why are there so many breaks indicated late in the dialogue?

2. What is Julie feeling? What, as a director or actor, would you want the audience to feel? Why?

3. In this monologue, the subtext is much more important than the text itself. What is Julie conveying through the subtext? How would you communicate this?

4. What can you tell about Julie's character in this scene? Through posture and stance, how could you help convey this?

5. How and when would you have Julie move in this cutting? Why?

Cuttings for Two Women

Two Gentlemen of Verona

Hedda Gabler

On Golden Pond

The Effect of Gamma Rays on
Man-in-the-Moon Marigolds

Antigone

Hedda Gabler
Photo by Barbara McLarney
Courtesy of Grossmont College Drama Department,
El Cajon, California

Act 1, scene 2

Two Gentlemen of Verona

William Shakespeare

T he play, unlike many of Shakespeare's others, is straightfor-
ward and not complicated by the addition of secondary plots.
Two Gentlemen of Verona has its basis in earlier story lines. In fact,
one of the most common plots in fiction and drama is how a faithless
companion makes love to the fiancée of his best friend.

There is disagreement over whether or not Shakespeare meant
the events of the play to be taken seriously. If taken on the level of
burlesque or quiet mockery of the convention of romantic love, the
play is more humorous.

In this cutting, which occurs early in the play, you can see that the
conversation between Julia and her "waiting-woman" seems to be
poking fun at the idea of falling in love. The action takes place in the
garden of Julia's house.

[*Enter* JULIA *and* LUCETTA.]

JULIA: But say, Lucetta, now we are alone,
  Wouldst thou, then, counsel me to fall in love?

LUCETTA: Aye, Madam, so you stumble not unheedfully.

JULIA: Of all the fair resort[1] of gentlemen
  That every day with parle[2] encounter me,
  In thy opinion which is worthiest love?

LUCETTA: Please you repeat their names, I'll show my mind
  According to my shallow simple skill.

JULIA: What think'st thou of the fair Sir Eglamour?

[1]resort: party or visitors   [2]parle: talk

LUCETTA: As of a knight well-spoken, neat and fine;
But, were I you, he never should be mine.

JULIA: What think'st thou of the rich Mercatio?

LUCETTA: Well of his wealth, but of himself, so so.

JULIA: What think'st thou of the gentle Proteus?

LUCETTA: Lord, Lord! To see what folly reigns in us!

JULIA: How now! What means this passion[3] at his name?

LUCETTA: Pardon, dear madam. 'Tis a passing shame
That I, unworthy body as I am,
Should censure[4] thus on lovely gentlemen.

JULIA: Why not on Proteus, as of all the rest?

LUCETTA: Then thus—of many good I think him best.

JULIA: Your reason?

LUCETTA: I have no other but a woman's reason.
I think him so, because I think him so.

JULIA: And wouldst thou have me cast my love on him?

LUCETTA: Aye, if you thought your love not cast away.

JULIA: Why, he, of all the rest, hath never moved[5] me.

LUCETTA: Yet he, of all the rest, I think, best loves ye.

JULIA: His little speaking shows his love but small.

LUCETTA: Fire that's closest kept burns most of all.

JULIA: They do not love that do not show their love.

LUCETTA: Oh, they love least that let men know their love.

JULIA: I would I knew his mind.

LUCETTA: Peruse this paper, madam.

JULIA: "To Julia."—Say, from whom?

LUCETTA: That the contents will show.

JULIA: Say, say, who gave it thee?

LUCETTA: Sir Valentine's page, and sent, I think, from Proteus.
He would have given it you, but I, being in the way,[6]

---

[3]passion: emotion [4]censure: criticize [5]moved: conversed with
[6]being in the way: meeting him

Did in your name receive it. Pardon the fault, pray.

JULIA: Now, by my modesty, a goodly broker![7]
Dare you presume to harbor wanton lines?
To whisper and conspire against my youth?
Now, trust me, 'tis an office of great worth,
And you an officer fit for the place.
There, take the paper. See it be returned,
Or else return no more into my sight.

LUCETTA: To plead for love deserves more fee than hate.

JULIA: Will ye be gone?

LUCETTA: That you may ruminate. [*Exit.*]

JULIA: And yet I would I had o'erlooked[8] the letter.
It were a shame to call her back again,
And pray her to[9] a fault for which I chid her.
What fool is she, that knows I am a maid
And would not force the letter to my view!
Since maids, in modesty, say "no" to that
Which they would have the profferer construe[10] "aye."
Fie, fie, how wayward is this foolish love
That, like a testy babe, will scratch the nurse,
And presently, all humbled, kiss the rod!
How churlishly I chid Lucetta hence,
When willingly I would have had her here!
How angerly I taught my brow to frown,
When inward joy enforced my heart to smile!
My penance is to call Lucetta back,
And ask remission for my folly past.
What ho! Lucetta!

[*Re-enter* LUCETTA.]

LUCETTA: What would your ladyship?

JULIA: Is 't near dinnertime?

LUCETTA: I would it were,
That you might kill your stomach[11] on your meat,[12]
And not upon your maid.

JULIA: What is 't that you took up so gingerly?

LUCETTA: Nothing.

[7]broker: go-between   [8]o'erlooked: read   [9]and pray her to: apologize for
[10]construe: translate   [11]stomach: both "anger" and "appetite"
[12]meat: pronounced "mate," therefore a pun

JULIA: Why didst thou stoop, then?

LUCETTA: To take a paper up that I let fall.

JULIA: And is that paper nothing?

LUCETTA: Nothing concerning me.

JULIA: Then let it lie for those that it concerns.

LUCETTA: Madam, it will not lie where it concerns
Unless it have a false interpreter.

JULIA: Some love of yours hath writ to you in rhyme.

LUCETTA: That I might sing it, madam, to a tune.
Give me a note. Your ladyship can set.[13]

JULIA: As little by such toys[14] as may be possible.
Best sing it to the tune of "Light o' love."[15]

LUCETTA: It is too heavy for so light a tune.

JULIA: Heavy! Belike it hath some burden,[16] then?

LUCETTA: Aye, and melodious were it, would you sing it.

JULIA: And why not you?

LUCETTA: I cannot reach so high.

JULIA: Let's see your song. How now, minion![17]

LUCETTA: Keep tune there still, so you will sing it out;
And yet methinks I do not like this tune.

JULIA: You do not?

LUCETTA: No, madam. It is too sharp.[18]

JULIA: You, minion, are too saucy.

LUCETTA: Nay, now you are too flat,
And mar the concord with too harsh a descant.[19]
There wanteth but a mean[20] to fill your song.

JULIA: The mean is drowned with your unruly bass.

LUCETTA: Indeed, I bid the base for Proteus.

---

[13]set: set it to music   [14]toys: trifles   [15]Light o'love: a well-known ditty
[16]burden: base part   [17]minion: hussy   [18]sharp: bitter
[19]descant: harmony   [20]mean: middle voice or melody in a song

JULIA: This babble shall not henceforth trouble me.
   Here is a coil[21] with protestation! [*Tears the letter.*]
   Go get you gone, and let the papers lie.
   You would be fingering them to anger me.

LUCETTA: She makes it strange, but she would be best pleased
   To be so angered with another letter. [*Exit.*]

JULIA: Nay, would I were so angered with the same!
   O hateful hands, to tear such loving words!
   Injurious wasps, to feed on such sweet honey,
   And kill the bees that yield it with your stings!
   I'll kiss each several paper[22] for amends.
   Look, here is writ "kind Julia." Unkind Julia!
   As in revenge of thy ingratitude,
   I throw thy name against the bruising stones,
   Trampling contemptuously on thy disdain.
   And here is writ "love-wounded Proteus."
   Poor wounded name! My bosom, as a bed,
   Shall lodge thee till thy wound be throughly healed,
   And thus I search[23] it with a sovereign kiss.
   But twice or thrice was "Proteus" written down.
   Be calm, good wind, blow not a word away
   Till I have found each letter in the letter,
   Except mine own name. That some whirlwind bear
   Unto a ragged, fearful-hanging rock,
   And throw it thence into the raging sea!
   Lo, here in one line is his name twice writ,
   "Poor forlorn Proteus, passionate Proteus,
   To the sweet Julia." That I'll tear away;
   And yet I will not, sith[24] so prettily
   He couples it to his complaining names.
   Thus will I fold them one upon another.
   Now kiss, embrace, contend, do what you will.

[*Re-enter* LUCETTA.]

LUCETTA: Madam,
   Dinner is ready, and your father stays.[25]

JULIA: Well, let us go.

LUCETTA: What, shall these papers lie like telltales here?

JULIA: If you respect them, best to take them up.

---

[21]coil: fuss   [22]several paper: separate piece   [23]search: probe
[24]sith: since   [25]stays: waits

LUCETTA: Nay, I was taken up[26] for laying them down.
Yet here they shall not lie for catching cold.

JULIA: I see you have a month's mind[27] to them.

LUCETTA: Aye, madam, you may say what sights you see.
I see things too, although you judge I wink.[28]

JULIA: Come, come. Will 't please you go?

[*Exeunt.*]

---

[26]taken up: blamed   [27]month's mind: longing   [28]wink: shut my eyes

Interpretation

1. This is not a serious play. How can you tell that from the lines?
What is the mood? How would you convey it?

2. What type of person is Julia? Lucetta? Justify your answers.

3. Draw a sketch of the setting you might like to use for this cutting. Why would you want it this way?

4. Indicate where and when you'd have the actors move. Justify the
moves.

5. What type of relationship do you think Julia and Lucetta have?
What makes you think so?

6. What are the most important lines in the cutting? Why are they
important? How can you convey them to an audience?

Act 1

Hedda Gabler

Henrik Ibsen

O ften considered the playwright's most perfectly written drama, *Hedda Gabler* is an excellent study in both character and format. Even though it was an international success when first presented in 1891, the play was highly criticized by those who believed that the heroine lacked motivation for the action she takes and that she has no redeeming features.

Hedda Gabler Tesman, the central character, is neurotic, self-centered, and maladjusted. Bored with life, she refuses even to acknowledge her own pregnancy. She has married a meek professor for security, not love. In this cutting Mrs. Elvsted comes to ask the Tesmans, Hedda and her husband, to watch over the brilliant but erratic young scholar, Eilert Lövberg. She is unaware that Hedda previously had brought about Lövberg's instability, now restored by Mrs. Elvsted.

Hedda is twenty-nine and Mrs. Elvsted a couple of years younger. The setting is "a spacious, handsome, and tastefully furnished drawing room."

Translated by William Archer

HEDDA [*Goes up to* MRS. ELVSTED, *smiles, and says in a low voice.*]: There. We have killed two birds with one stone.

MRS. ELVSTED: What do you mean?

HEDDA: Could you not see that I wanted him to go?

MRS. ELVSTED: Yes, to write the letter—

HEDDA: And that I might speak to you alone.

MRS. ELVSTED [*Confused.*]: About the same thing?

HEDDA: Precisely.

Mrs. Elvsted [*Apprehensively.*]: But there is nothing more, Mrs. Tesman! Absolutely nothing!

Hedda: Oh, yes, but there is. There is a great deal more—I can see that. Sit here—and we'll have a cosy, confidential chat. [*She forces Mrs. Elvsted to sit in the easy-chair beside the stove, and seats herself on one of the footstools.*]

Mrs. Elvsted [*Anxiously, looking at her watch.*]: But, my dear Mrs. Tesman—I was really on the point of going.

Hedda: Oh, you can't be in such a hurry.—Well? Now tell me something about your life at home.

Mrs. Elvsted: Oh, that is just what I care least to speak about.

Hedda: But to me, dear—? Why, weren't we school-fellows?

Mrs. Elvsted: Yes, but you were in the class above me. Oh, how dreadfully afraid of you I was then!

Hedda: Afraid of me?

Mrs. Elvsted: *Yes,* dreadfully. For when we met on the stairs you used always to pull my hair.

Hedda: Did I, really?

Mrs. Elvsted: Yes, and once you said you would burn it off my head.

Hedda: Oh, that was all nonsense, of course.

Mrs. Elvsted: Yes, but I was so silly in those days.—And since then, too—we have drifted so far—far apart from each other. Our circles have been so entirely different.

Hedda: Well then, we must try to drift together again. Now listen! At school we said *du* to each other; and we called each other by our Christian names—

Mrs. Elvsted: No, I am sure you must be mistaken.

Hedda: No, not at all! I can remember quite distinctly. So now we are going to renew our old friendship. [*Draws the footstool closer to Mrs. Elvsted.*] There now! [*Kisses her cheek.*] You must say *du* to me and call me Hedda.

Mrs. Elvsted [*Presses and pats her hands.*]: Oh, how good and kind you are! I am not used to such kindness.

Hedda: There, there, there! And I shall say *du* to you, as in the old days, and call you my dear Thora.

Hedda Gabler
Photo courtesy of Kent State University Theatre, Kent, Ohio

MRS. ELVSTED: My name is Thea.

HEDDA: Why, of course! I meant Thea. [*Looks at her compassionately.*] So you are not accustomed to goodness and kindness, Thea? Not in your own home?

MRS. ELVSTED: Oh, if I only had a home! But I haven't any; I have never had a home.

HEDDA [*Looks at her for a moment.*]: I almost suspected as much.

MRS. ELVSTED [*Gazing helplessly before her.*]: Yes—yes—yes.

HEDDA: I don't quite remember—was it not as housekeeper that you first went to Mr. Elvsted's?

MRS. ELVSTED: I really went as governess. But his wife—his late wife—was an invalid,—and rarely left her room. So I had to look after the housekeeping as well.

HEDDA: And then—at last—you became mistress of the house.

MRS. ELVSTED [*Sadly.*]: Yes, I did.

HEDDA: Let me see—about how long ago was that?

MRS. ELVSTED: My marriage?

HEDDA: Yes.

MRS. ELVSTED: Five years ago.

HEDDA: To be sure; it must be that.

MRS. ELVSTED: Oh, those five years—! Or at all events the last two or three of them! Oh, if you[1] could only imagine—

HEDDA [*Giving her a little slap on the hand.*]: *De?* Fie, Thea!

MRS. ELVSTED: Yes, yes, I will try—Well if—you could only imagine and understand—

HEDDA [*Lightly.*]: Eilert Lövborg has been in your neighborhood about three years, hasn't he?

MRS. ELVSTED [*Looks at her doubtfully.*]: Eilert Lövborg? Yes—he has.

HEDDA: Had you known him before, in town here?

MRS. ELVSTED: Scarcely at all. I mean—I knew him by name of course.

HEDDA: But you saw a good deal of him in the country?

MRS. ELVSTED: Yes, he came to us every day. You see, he gave the children lessons; for in the long run I couldn't manage it all myself.

HEDDA: No, that's clear.—And your husband—? I suppose he is often away from home?

MRS. ELVSTED: Yes. Being Sheriff, you know, he has to travel about a good deal in his district.

HEDDA [*Leaning against the arm of the chair.*]: Thea—my poor, sweet Thea—now you must tell me everything—exactly as it stands.

MRS. ELVSTED: Well, then, you must question me.

---

[1]Mrs. Elvsted here uses the formal pronoun *De,* whereupon Hedda rebukes her. In her next speech Mrs. Elvsted says *du.*

HEDDA: What sort of a man is your husband, Thea? I mean—you know—in everyday life. Is he kind to you?

MRS. ELVSTED [*Evasively.*]: I am sure he means well in everything.

HEDDA: I should think he must be altogether too old for you. There is at least twenty years' difference between you, is there not?

MRS. ELVSTED [*Irritably.*]: Yes, that is true, too. Everything about him is repellent to me! We have not a thought in common. We have no single point of sympathy—he and I.

HEDDA: But is he not fond of you all the same? In his own way?

MRS. ELVSTED: Oh, I really don't know. I think he regards me simply as a useful property. And then it doesn't cost much to keep me. I am not expensive.

HEDDA: That is stupid of you.

MRS. ELVSTED [*Shakes her head.*]: It cannot be otherwise—not with him. I don't think he really cares for anyone but himself—and perhaps a little for the children.

HEDDA: And for Eilert Lövborg, Thea.

MRS. ELVSTED [*Looking at her.*]: For Eilert Lövborg? What puts that into your head?

HEDDA: Well, my dear—I should say, when he sends you after him all the way to town—[*Smiling almost imperceptibly.*] And besides, you said so yourself, to Tesman.

MRS. ELVSTED [*With a little nervous twitch.*]: Did I? Yes, I suppose I did. [*Vehemently, but not loudly.*] No—I may just as well make a clean breast of it at once! For it must all come out in any case.

HEDDA: Why, my dear Thea—?

MRS. ELVSTED: Well, to make a long story short: My husband did not know that I was coming.

HEDDA: What! Your husband didn't know it!

MRS. ELVSTED: No, of course not. For that matter, he was away from home himself—he was traveling. Oh, I could bear it no longer, Hedda! I couldn't indeed—so utterly alone as I should have been in future.

HEDDA: Well? And then?

MRS. ELVSTED: So I put together some of my things—what I needed most—as quietly as possible. And then I left the house.

HEDDA: Without a word?

MRS. ELVSTED: Yes—and took the train straight to town.

HEDDA: Why, my dear, good Thea—to think of you daring to do it!

MRS. ELVSTED [*Rises and moves about the room.*]: What else could I possibly do?

HEDDA: But what do you think your husband will say when you go home again?

MRS. ELVSTED [*At the table, looks at her.*]: Back to him.

HEDDA: Of course.

MRS. ELVSTED: I shall never go back to him again.

HEDDA [*Rising and going towards her.*]: Then you have left your home—for good and all?

MRS. ELVSTED: Yes. There was nothing else to be done.

HEDDA: But then—to take flight so openly.

MRS. ELVSTED: Oh, it's impossible to keep things of that sort secret.

HEDDA: But what do you think people will say of you, Thea?

MRS. ELVSTED: They may say what they like for aught *I* care. [*Seats herself wearily and sadly on the sofa.*] I have done nothing but what I had to do.

HEDDA [*After a short silence.*]: And what are your plans now? What do you think of doing?

MRS. ELVSTED: I don't know yet. I only know this, that I must live here, where Eilert Lövborg is—if I am to live at all.

HEDDA [*Takes a chair from the table, seats herself beside her, and strokes her hand.*]: My dear Thea—how did this—this friendship—between you and Eilert Lövborg come about?

MRS. ELVSTED: Oh, it grew up gradually. I gained a sort of influence over him.

HEDDA: Indeed?

MRS. ELVSTED: He gave up his old habits. Not because I asked him to, for I never dared do that. But of course he saw how repulsive they were to me; and so he dropped them.

HEDDA [*Concealing an involuntary smile of scorn.*]: Then you have reclaimed him—as the saying goes—my little Thea.

MRS. ELVSTED: So he says himself, at any rate. And he, on his side, has made a real human being of me—taught me to think, and to understand so many things.

HEDDA: Did he give you lessons too, then?

MRS. ELVSTED: No, not exactly lessons. But he talked to me— talked about such an infinity of things. And then came the lovely, happy time when I began to share in his work—when he allowed me to help him!

HEDDA: Oh, he did, did he?

MRS. ELVSTED: Yes! He never wrote anything without my assistance.

HEDDA: You were two good comrades, in fact?

MRS. ELVSTED [*Eagerly.*]: Comrades! Yes, fancy, Hedda—that is the very word he used!—Oh, I ought to feel perfectly happy; and yet I cannot; for I don't know how long it will last.

HEDDA: Are you no surer of him than that?

MRS. ELVSTED [*Gloomily.*]: A woman's shadow stands between Eilert Lövborg and me.

HEDDA [*Looks at her anxiously.*]: Who can that be?

MRS. ELVSTED: I don't know. Some one he knew in his—in his past. Some one he has never been able wholly to forget.

HEDDA: What has he told you—about this?

MRS. ELVSTED: He has only once—quite vaguely—alluded to it.

HEDDA: Well! And what did he say?

MRS. ELVSTED: He said that when they parted, she threatened to shoot him with a pistol.

HEDDA [*With cold composure.*]: Oh, nonsense! No one does that sort of thing here.

MRS. ELVSTED: No. And that is why I think it must have been that red-haired singing woman whom he once—

HEDDA: Yes, very likely.

MRS. ELVSTED: For I remember they used to say of her that she carried loaded firearms.

HEDDA: Oh—then of course it must have been she.

MRS. ELVSTED [*Wringing her hands.*]: And now just fancy, Hedda—
I hear that this singing-woman—that she is in town again!
Oh, I don't know what to do—

HEDDA [*Glancing towards the inner room.*]: Hush! Here comes
Tesman. [*Rises and whispers.*] Thea—all this must remain
between you and me.

Interpretation

1. What sort of woman is Hedda? What are her most important
traits? How can you tell? Is there any motivation for her behavior? If
so, what is it?

2. Why would you either like or dislike playing or directing this
scene?

3. What can you tell about Mrs. Elvsted? Contrast her character
with Hedda's. How does she perceive the relationship with Hedda?
How do you want the audience to perceive it?

4. How could you use stance, movement, and voice to convey Hedda's character? Mrs. Elvsted's?

5. What are the most important ideas expressed in this cutting?
Why do you think so? How would you point them up for an audience?

6. What is the subtext you would want the audience to grasp?

Act 2, scene 1

On Golden Pond

Ernest Thompson

For the last fifty years, Ethel and Norman Thayer have spent their summers vacationing on Golden Pond. A retired professor nearing eighty, Norman has a caustic wit, heart problems, and a failing memory.

The Thayers' daughter, Chelsea, has just come back from a European trip with her dentist boyfriend, Bill. His son, Billy, stayed with the Thayers while Chelsea and Bill were gone. Despite ominous beginnings, he and the Thayers, especially Norman, have come to appreciate each other.

Approaching the house as she returns for Billy, Chelsea hears her mother singing familiar old camp tunes, reminding her of her growing-up years on Golden Pond. Her memories obviously are different from those Billy will have.

The action takes place in a large, old living room.

ETHEL: How'd you get here?

CHELSEA: I rented a car. A Volare. It's made by Plymouth. I got it from Avis. [*She walks to* ETHEL. *They embrace.*] They *do* try hard.

ETHEL: You're not supposed to come till the fifteenth.

CHELSEA: Today's the fifteenth.

ETHEL: No!

CHELSEA: 'Fraid so.

ETHEL: Well. No wonder you're here.

CHELSEA: Still have the kid or did you drown him?

ETHEL: Still have him.

CHELSEA: Are he and Norman asleep?

ETHEL: You must be joking. They're out on the lake already, antagonizing the fish. Still have Bill or did you drown him?

CHELSEA: Still got him. But he's not with me. He went back to the coast. He had a mouth that needed looking into.

ETHEL: Oh. You must have left Boston at the crack of dawn.

CHELSEA: I left Boston in the middle of the night. I felt like driving. I didn't feel like getting lost, but it worked out that way.

ETHEL: If you'd come more often, you wouldn't get lost.

CHELSEA: You're right. If I promise to come more often will you give me a cup of coffee?

ETHEL: All right. I could do that. Yes. You must have had a lovely time in Europe. You look wonderful. [*She exits into the kitchen.*]

CHELSEA: I do? I did. I had a lovely time. [*Peers out at the lake.*]

ETHEL [*Offstage.*]: I always thought Norman and I should travel, but we never got to it somehow. I'm not sure Norman would like Europe.

CHELSEA: He wouldn't like Italy.

ETHEL [*Offstage.*]: No?

CHELSEA: Too many Italians.

ETHEL [*Enters.*]: I've got the perker going. See the boys?

CHELSEA: Yes. What are they doing out there? It's starting to rain.

ETHEL: Ah, well. I told Norman not to go. The loons have been calling for it. I'm afraid Norman doesn't give them much credence.

CHELSEA: They're going to get drenched.

ETHEL: I think between the two of them they have sense enough to come in out of the rain. At least I hope they do. [*A moment passes as they look out at the lake.*] Isn't it beautiful?

CHELSEA [*She nods and looks at* ETHEL.]: Look at you. You've had that robe for as long as I can remember.

ETHEL [*She tries to arrange it.*]: It looks like it, doesn't it?

CHELSEA: It looks great. [*She stares at* ETHEL, *moved. She steps to her and hugs her emphatically.*]

ETHEL: You're in a huggy mood today. What's the matter?

CHELSEA: You seem different.

ETHEL: You mean old.

CHELSEA: I don't know.

ETHEL: Well, that's what happens if you live long enough. You end up being old. It's one of the disadvantages of a long life. I still prefer it to the alternative.

CHELSEA: How does it really make you feel?

ETHEL: Not much different. A little more aware of the sunrises, I guess. And the sunsets.

CHELSEA: It makes *me* mad.

ETHEL: Ah, well, it doesn't exactly make me want to jump up and down. [CHELSEA *hugs* ETHEL *again*]. Oh, dear. They're not digging the grave yet. Come sit down. You must be exhausted. [ETHEL *sits.* CHELSEA *wanders.*]

CHELSEA: Have Billy and Norman gotten along all right?

ETHEL: Billy is the happiest thing that's happened to Norman since Roosevelt. I should have rented him a thirteen-year-old boy years ago.

CHELSEA: You could have traded me in. [ETHEL *laughs.*] Billy reminds me of myself out there, way back when. Except I think he makes a better son than I did.

ETHEL: Well, you made a very nice daughter.

CHELSEA: Does Billy put the worm on the hook by himself?

ETHEL: I'm really not sure.

CHELSEA: I hope so. You lose points if you throw up, I remember that. I always apologized to those nice worms before I impaled them. Well, they'll get even with me some day, won't they?

ETHEL: You're beginning to sound an awful lot like your father.

CHELSEA: Uh oh. [*Changing direction.*] Thank you for taking care of Billy.

ETHEL: Thank *you.* I'm glad it gives us another chance to see you. Plus, it's been a tremendous education. Norman's vocabulary will never be the same but that's all right.

CHELSEA [*Turning to the mantel and picking up a picture.*]: Look at this. Chelsea on the swim team. That was a great exercise in humiliation.

ETHEL: Oh, stop it. You were a good diver.

CHELSEA: I wasn't a good diver. I was a good sport. I could never do a damn back flip.

ETHEL: Well, we were proud of you for trying.

CHELSEA: Right. Everyone got a big splash out of me trying. Why do you think I subjected myself to all that? I wasn't aiming for the 1956 Olympics, you know. I was just trying to please Norman. Because he'd been a diver, in the eighteen hundreds.

ETHEL: Can't you be home for five minutes without getting started on the past?

CHELSEA: This house seems to set me off.

ETHEL: Well, it shouldn't. It's a nice house.

CHELSEA: I act like a big person everywhere else. I do. I'm in charge in Los Angeles. I guess I've never grown up on Golden Pond. Do you understand?

ETHEL: I don't think so.

CHELSEA: It doesn't matter. There's just something about coming back here that makes me feel like a little fat girl.

ETHEL: Sit down and tell me about your trip.

CHELSEA [*An outburst.*]: I don't want to sit down. Where were you all that time? You never bailed me out.

ETHEL: I didn't know you needed bailing out.

CHELSEA: Well, I did.

ETHEL: Here we go again. You had a miserable childhood. Your father was overbearing, your mother ignored you. What else is new? Don't you think everyone looks back on their childhood with some bitterness or regret about something? You are a big girl now, aren't you tired of it all? You have this unpleasant chip on your shoulder which is very unattractive. You only come home when I beg you to, and when you get here all you can do is be disagreeable about the past. Life marches by, Chelsea, I suggest you get on with it. [ETHEL *stands and glares at* CHELSEA.] You're such a nice person. Can't you think of something nice to say?

CHELSEA: I married Bill in Brussels.

ETHEL: You did what in Brussels?

CHELSEA: I married Bill.

ETHEL: Does it count in this country?

CHELSEA: 'Fraid so.

ETHEL [*Stepping to* CHELSEA *and kissing her.*]: Well, bless you. Congratulations.

CHELSEA: Thank you.

ETHEL: You have an odd way of building up to good news.

CHELSEA: I know.

ETHEL: Bill seems very nice.

CHELSEA: He's better than nice. He's an adult, too. I decided to go for an adult marriage this time. It's a standard five-year contract with renewable options. If it doesn't work out I still get to keep my gold caps.

ETHEL: What about Billy?

CHELSEA: Bill gets to keep Billy.

ETHEL: Will Billy live with you?

CHELSEA: Yes. That's part of the reason Bill had to get back to LA. He's murdering his ex-wife. She doesn't want the kid anyway.

ETHEL: Do you?

CHELSEA: Yes.

ETHEL: Well, I'm so pleased.

CHELSEA: Nothing to it. I'm twice as old as you were when you married Norman. Think that means anything?

ETHEL: I hope it means that Bill will be only half as much trouble. Norman will be so surprised.

CHELSEA: I'll bet.

ETHEL: All he wants is for you to be happy.

CHELSEA: Could have fooled me. He always makes me feel like I've got my shoes on the wrong feet.

ETHEL: That's just his manner. He enjoys keeping people on their toes.

CHELSEA: I'm glad *he* gets pleasure out of it.

ETHEL: Dear God, how long do you plan to keep this up? Hmm?

CHELSEA: I don't know. I . . . can't talk to him. I've never been able to.

ETHEL: Have you ever *tried?*

CHELSEA: Yes, we've discussed the relative stupidity of Puerto Rican baseball players. I don't even know him.

ETHEL: Well, he'll be along any minute. I'll be happy to introduce you. You don't get to know a person by staying away for years at a time.

CHELSEA: I know. Maybe someday we can try to be friends.

ETHEL: Chelsea, Norman is eighty years old. He has heart palpitations and a problem remembering things. When exactly do you expect this friendship to begin?

CHELSEA: I don't know. . . . I'm afraid of him.

ETHEL: Well, he's afraid of you. You should get along fine.

Interpretation

1. What is Chelsea like? What are her most important traits? How does she feel about her parents? Why?

2. What type of person is Ethel? How does she feel about Chelsea? What does she think about the way Chelsea views her father?

3. What is the central idea of this cutting? Explain. What is the prevailing mood?

4. What sort of relationship do the two women have? Who is the dominant character? Why do you think so?

5. What provides the conflict in this cutting? Is it resolved? Explain.

6. What type of setting would you use? How would you block this scene? Why?

The Effect of Gamma Rays on Man-in-the-Moon Marigolds

Paul Zindel

The major characters are a mother and two daughters. The mother, whose husband left years before, is lonely, frustrated, and suffering emotional distress. Desperately unhappy, she takes out her feelings on her two daughters, also embarrassing them with her eccentric way of dressing.

Ruth, the older and prettier of the two girls, is very high-strung and temperamental, unable to match her sister Tillie's scholastic achievements. Tillie tries to escape her unhappy home life by immersing herself completely into scientific experimentation.

Zindel, who wrote the play when he was just twenty-five, says that he "suspects" it is autobiographical.

In the following cutting, Tillie is getting ready to accept an award for her experiment with man-in-the-moon marigolds. Ruth, who is jealous of Tillie's achievement, tries her best to upset her and ruin the evening.

The action is set in "a room of wood which was once a vegetable store." On a table stands "a large three-panel screen," on which Tillie's experiment is listed and described.

RUTH: The only competition you have to worry about is Janice Vickery. They say she caught it near Princess Bay Boulevard and it was still alive when she took the skin off it.

TILLIE [*Taking some plants from* RUTH.]: Let me do that, please, Ruth.

RUTH: I'm sorry I touched them, really.

TILLIE: Why don't you feed Peter?

RUTH: Because I don't feel like feeding him . . . Now I feel like feeding him. [*She gets some lettuce from a bag.*] I heard that it screamed for three minutes after she put it in because the water wasn't boiling yet. How much talent does it take to boil the skin off a cat and then stick the bones together again? That's what I want to know. Ugh. I had a dream about that, too. I figure she did it in less than a day and she ends up as one of the top five winners . . . and you spend months growing atomic flowers.

TILLIE: Don't you think you should finish getting ready?

RUTH: Finish? This is it!

TILLIE: Are you going to wear that sweater?

RUTH: Look, don't worry about me. I'm not getting up on any stage, and if I did I wouldn't be caught dead with a horrible bow like that.

TILLIE: Mother put it—

RUTH: They're going to laugh you off the stage again like when you cranked that atom in assembly . . . I didn't mean that . . . The one they're going to laugh at is Mama.

TILLIE: What?

RUTH: I said the one they're going to laugh at is Mama . . . Oh, let me take that bow off.

TILLIE: It's all right.

RUTH: Look, just sit still. I don't want everybody making fun of you.

TILLIE: What made you say that about Mama?

RUTH: Oh, I heard them talking in the Science Office yesterday. Mr. Goodman and Miss Hanley. She's getting $12.63 to chaperon the thing tonight.

TILLIE: What were they saying?

RUTH: Miss Hanley was telling Mr. Goodman about Mama . . . when she found out you were one of the five winners. And he wanted to know if there was something wrong with Mama because she sounded crazy over the phone. And Miss Hanley said she *was* crazy and she always has been crazy and she can't wait to see what she looks like after all these years. Miss Hanley said her nickname used to be *Betty the Loon.*

TILLIE [*As* RUTH *combs her hair.*]: Ruth, you're hurting me.

RUTH: She was just like you and everybody thought she was a big weirdo. There! You look much better! [*She goes back to the rabbit.*] Peter, if anybody stuck you in a pot of boiling water I'd kill them, do you know that? . . . [*Then to* TILLIE.] What do they call boiling the skin off a cat? I call it murder, that's what I call it. They say it was hit by a car and Janice just scooped it up and before you could say *bingo* it was screaming in a pot of boiling water . . .

Do you know what they're all waiting to see? Mama's feathers! That's what Miss Hanley said. She said Mama blabs as though she was the Queen of England and just as proper as can be, and that her idea of getting dressed up is to put on all the feathers in the world and go as a bird. Always trying to get somewhere, like a great big bird.

TILLIE: Don't tell Mama, please. It doesn't matter.

RUTH: I was up there watching her getting dressed and sure enough, she's got the feathers out.

TILLIE: You didn't tell her what Miss Hanley said?

RUTH: Are you kidding? I just told her I didn't like the feathers and I didn't think she should wear any. But I'll bet she doesn't listen to me.

TILLIE: It doesn't matter.

RUTH: It doesn't matter? Do you think I want to be laughed right out of the school tonight, with Chris Burns there, and all? Laughed right out of the school, with your electric hair and her feathers on that stage, and Miss Hanley splitting her sides?

TILLIE: Promise me you won't say anything.

RUTH: On one condition.

TILLIE: What?

RUTH: Give Peter to me.

TILLIE [*Ignoring her.*]: The taxi will be here any minute and I won't have all this stuff ready. Did you see my speech?

RUTH: I mean it. Give Peter to me.

TILLIE: He belongs to all of us.

RUTH: For me. All for me. What do you care? He doesn't mean anything to you anymore, now that you've got all those crazy plants.

TILLIE: Will you stop?

RUTH: If you don't give him to me I'm going to tell Mama that everybody's waiting to laugh at her.

TILLIE: Where are those typewritten cards?

RUTH: I MEAN IT! Give him to me!

TILLIE: Does he mean that much to you?

RUTH: Yes!

TILLIE: All right.

RUTH [*After a burst of private laughter.*]: Betty the Loon . . . [*She laughs again.*] That's what they used to call her, you know. Betty the Loon!

TILLIE: I don't think that's very nice.

RUTH: First they had Betty the Loon, and now they've got Tillie the Loon . . . [*To rabbit.*] You don't have to worry about me turning you in for any old plants . . .

How much does a taxi cost from here to the school?

TILLIE: Not much.

RUTH: I wish she'd give me the money it costs for a taxi—and for all that cardboard and paint and flowerpots and stuff. The only time she ever made a fuss over me was when she drove me nuts.

TILLIE: Tell her to hurry, please.

RUTH: By the way, I went over to see Janice Vickery's pot, that she did you know what in, and I started telling her and her mother about the worms in Mr. Alexander Brougham's legs, and I got thrown out because it was too near dinner time. That Mrs. Vickery kills me. She can't stand worms in somebody else's legs but she lets her daughter cook a cat.

Interpretation

1. Why do you think Ruth keeps needling Tillie? Why does she want to upset her?

2. Is Ruth a likeable person? Tillie? Why or why not? How do you feel about them? How would you like an audience to feel?

3. What sort of atmosphere would you want to create with this cutting? Why?

4. Who is the dominant character? Why do you think so? How would you emphasize this?

5. How would you block this cutting?

6. What emotions are the two girls feeling? Why? How would you communicate this to the audience?

7. What is the central idea of this cutting?

Prologue

Antigone

Sophocles

Written about 441 BC, this play deals with the conflict between
moral rights and state's rights.

After a battle in which Thebes has defeated the enemy but lost its
king, the new monarch Creon decrees that the body of Polyneices,
the unsuccessful invader, will remain unburied. Furthermore, anyone caught attempting to bury the body will be put to death.

No sooner has the decree been issued than Antigone, Creon's niece
and the sister of Polyneices, attempts to bury her brother. She makes
no attempt to hide what she's done. In fact, she challenges Creon's
right to issue the edict, since it's plainly against the will of the gods.

This cutting opens the action and occurs in front of Creon's palace.

Translated by Dudley Fitts and Robert Fitzgerald

[ANTIGONE *and* ISMENE *enter from the central door of the palace.*]

ANTIGONE: Ismene, dear sister,
　　You would think that we had already suffered enough
　　For the curse on Oedipus:
　　I cannot imagine any grief
　　That you and I have not gone through. And now—
　　Have they told you the new decree of our King Creon?

ISMENE: I have heard nothing: I know
　　That two sisters lost two brothers, a double death
　　In a single hour; and I know that the Argive army
　　Fled in the night; but beyond this, nothing.

ANTIGONE: I thought so. And that is why I wanted you
　　To come out here with me. There is something we must do.

ISMENE: Why do you speak so strangely?

ANTIGONE: Listen, Ismene:
　　Creon buried our brother Eteocles
　　With military honors, gave him a soldier's funeral,
　　And it was right that he should; but Polyneices,
　　Who fought as bravely and died as miserably,—
　　They say that Creon has sworn
　　No one shall bury him, no one mourn for him,
　　But his body must lie in the fields, a sweet treasure
　　For carrion birds to find as they search for food.
　　That is what they say, and our good Creon is coming here
　　To announce it publicly; and the penalty—
　　Stoning to death in the public square!
　　There it is,
　　And now you can prove what you are:
　　A true sister, or a traitor to your family.

ISMENE: Antigone, you are mad! What could I possibly do?

ANTIGONE: You must decide whether you will help me or not.

ISMENE: I do not understand you. Help you in what!

ANTIGONE: Ismene, I am going to bury him. Will you come?

ISMENE: Bury him! You have just said the new law forbids it.

ANTIGONE: He is my brother. And he is your brother, too.

ISMENE: But think of the danger! Think what Creon will do!

ANTIGONE: Creon is not strong enough to stand in my way.

ISMENE: Ah sister!
　　Oedipus died, everyone hating him
　　For what his own search brought to light, his eyes
　　Ripped out by his own hand; and Iocaste died,
　　His mother and wife at once: she twisted the cords
　　That strangled her life; and our two brothers died,
　　Each killed by the other's sword. And we are left:
　　But oh, Antigone,
　　Think how much more terrible than these
　　Our own death would be if we should go against Creon
　　And do what he has forbidden! We are only women,
　　We cannot fight with men, Antigone!
　　The law is strong, we must give in to the law
　　In this thing, and in worse. I beg the dead
　　To forgive me, but I am helpless: I must yield

To those in authority. And I think it is dangerous business
To be always meddling.

ANTIGONE: If that is what you think,
I should not want you, even if you asked to come.
You have made your choice, and can be what you want to be.
But I will bury him; and if I must die,
I say that this crime is holy: I shall lie down
With him in death, and I shall be as dear
To him as he to me.
It is the dead,
Not the living, who make the longest demands:
We die for ever . . .
You may do as you like,
Since apparently the laws of the gods mean nothing to you.

ISMENE: They mean a great deal to me; but I have no strength
To break laws that were made for the public good.

ANTIGONE: That must be your excuse, I suppose. But as for me,
I will bury the brother I love.

ISMENE: Antigone,
I am so afraid for you!

ANTIGONE: You need not be:
You have yourself to consider, after all.

ISMENE: But no one must hear of this, you must tell no one!
I will keep it a secret, I promise!

ANTIGONE: Oh tell it! Tell everyone!
Think how they'll hate you when it all comes out
If they learn that you knew about it all the time!

ISMENE: So fiery! You should be cold with fear.

ANTIGONE: Perhaps. But I am doing only what I must.

ISMENE: But can you do it? I say that you cannot.

ANTIGONE: Very well: when my strength gives out, I shall do no
more.

ISMENE: Impossible things should not be tried at all.

ANTIGONE: Go away, Ismene:
I shall be hating you soon, and the dead will too,
For your words are hateful. Leave me my foolish plan:
I am not afraid of the danger; if it means death,
It will not be the worst of deaths—death without honor.

ISMENE: Go then, if you feel that you must.
  You are unwise,
  But a loyal friend indeed to those who love you.
  [*Exit into the palace.* ANTIGONE *goes off, left.*]

Interpretation

1. How would you characterize Antigone? Ismene?

2. Why do you think Antigone is so determined to bury her brother?

3. What provides the conflict in this cutting? Is it between Antigone and Ismene? Why do you think so?

4. What type of costumes would you have the sisters wear? Why? What type of set would you design?

5. What is the prevailing mood of this cutting? What would you as director or actor want the audience to feel while viewing it? Afterwards? Why?

CUTTINGS FOR TWO MEN

Blue Earth

Othello, The Moor of Venice

A Thousand Clowns

Two Gentlemen of Verona

The Way of the World

Blue Earth
Photo courtesy of Kent State
University Theatre, Kent, Ohio

Blue Earth

Arthur Winfield Knight

Jim and Cole Younger are brothers who rode with Jesse and Frank James. They have served twenty-five-year prison terms and now are on probation. Jim has fallen in love with Alice, who also loves him. She became interested in him while he was in prison and used to visit him there. Yet, the relationship is doomed in that they come from different backgrounds—the Youngers, poor men who became outlaws, Alice from "one of the best families in St. Paul." Jim's parole board also has forbidden them to marry.

Alice has just left Jim's hotel room, probably for the last time. The room is in the Reardon Hotel in St. Paul, Minnesota; it is October 19, 1902. Jim is in his early fifties, Cole four years older. Cole entered the room just before she left.

JIM [*Stupidly.*]: She's gone.

COLE: Maybe it's just as well.

JIM [*Angrily.*]: What do you mean?

COLE: You'd never fit into *that* kind of life, Jim. She's always had money, opportunity. *Everything.* [*Cryptically.*] Whether you're rich or poor, it's a good thing to have money.

JIM: Huh?

COLE: How are you going to support her stocking shelves in a grocery store?

JIM: It's no worse than selling tombstones.

COLE [*Laughing.*]: *I* don't have to support her. [*Trying to turn the conversation around.*] Everybody used to tell me I could accomplish great things, even that doctor who felt the bumps on our heads when we were in Stillwater.[1] Doctor Morris kept

[1]Stillwater: the state prison

measuring my skull with calipers and taking notes and looking real serious, mumbling to himself, and finally he said, "Mr. Younger, you're a natural leader." I just looked at him and said, "Doc, if everything you say is true, how come I'm here?"

[COLE *almost roars with laughter—he is one of those men who loves his own jokes—but* JIM *doesn't even smile as he sits on the edge of the bed. He holds his hands to his head, and when* COLE *notices how morose he is,* COLE's *laughter suddenly subsides.*]

I guess it wasn't as funny as I thought.

JIM: It's OK. I know I'm not right for Alice better than you do. I'm 30 years older, and my future was already behind me by the time she was born; but *that doesn't stop me from loving her . . .* wanting her.

COLE [*Suddenly serious.*]: I know how you feel. During the war, I killed enough blue bellies to keep a tombstone company in business, so it seems ironic that I ended up selling monuments . . . I've studied religion, philosophy, everything, trying to find answers, but the only one I keep comin' up with is that I'm a loser. This is just my karma, like it or not. It's the way the cards were dealt out to me.

JIM [*Not as resigned as* COLE.]: It was a dirty deal. Both of us got dead man's hands, like Hickok, but we're still trying to pretend we're alive. We go through the motions.

COLE: I keep telling myself I might *really* come back to life if I pretend to be alive long enough. If I make the motions. . . . I try to take pleasure in the little things: a cup of coffee—I hated that tea they always served us in Stillwater—a good cigar . . . I went to a smoker the other night at the Elks Hall in Minneapolis. [*Becoming animated. Flushed.*] You should have seen some of the tricks the gal there performed. She called herself an exotic dancer. [*Whistling.*] We never had entertainment like that back home.

JIM: Once I found Alice, I wasn't interested in what other women were doing anymore.

COLE [*Gently.*]: Alice is gone now.

JIM: Yeah.

[COLE *takes the pistol out of the holster, examining the gun closely, sighting along the barrel.*]

COLE: This is a fine-looking weapon, but your parole officer would have you back in prison if he knew you had it.

JIM: My parole officer isn't here.

COLE: Why did you buy it?

JIM: Maybe because it's forbidden. [*Getting up from the bed, pacing.*] I don't know.

COLE: Do you ever miss the old days?

[*As he says this, he puts the pistol alongside his leg, as if it were holstered, then he pretends to draw it. He is still remarkably fast.*]

JIM: They were all I thought about until Alice came along. I was almost obsessed with returning to Lee's Summit. I kept trying to imagine what it would be like living near Frank again.

COLE: The lucky bastard never served a day in prison.

JIM: I've read that he has a nice string of horses, and that he's racing them at fairs.

COLE: I've even heard that people will come up to him, asking for his autograph. He's become a hero. He's even charging them 50 cents if they want to take a look at the place where he and Jesse grew up.

JIM: He's probably making more than we did sticking up trains.

COLE [*Laughing.*]: He finally found a way to make crime pay.

[*He holds the pisol as if he were firing it.*]

Sometimes I think we ought to blast our way out of here—we belong in Missouri—but I know they'd come after us. . . . And I don't have the energy I used to. The only thing that's "young" about us now is our name.

[COLE *crouches, fanning the pistol, and you can hear the hammer click rapidly.*]

JIM: At least they can't take our memories away . . . but I'll bet they'd like to.

COLE: I try not to be too bitter. What good does it do?

JIM: When I was wounded at Lawrence and Quantrell wanted to kill me because I was slowing the others down, I remember you called him "a cold-hearted devil" and said, "I'll stay with Jim and fight until the end, then carry him on my shoulders until I fall." I never saw him back down before another man. . . . I don't know that I ever really thanked you.

COLE: You didn't have to. [*Putting the gun back into the holster.*]

JIM: Lawrence was the one place I was kind of ashamed to be. . . . The killing just got out of hand.

COLE: Regret's a wasted emotion. . . . It doesn't change anything.

JIM: I know. [*Passionately.*] But I can still see all those people runnin' out into the street. Still hear them screaming. It seemed like the whole town was burning. The flames must have been a hundred feet high.

[JIM *sits on the bed again, heavily, as if the memory of what happened has worn him out.*]

COLE [*Coming toward the front of the stage.*]: You never killed a man who didn't need it—or who wasn't wearing a uniform with a different color than your own. . . . You always tried to protect women. And you never took money from a Confederate, a brother, when the war was over. . . . There's a day coming when the secrets of all hearts will be laid open before the All-seeing eye, and every act of our lives will be scrutinized; when that happens, I know you'll come out clean. . . . We did what we thought was right, which is more than most people can say. I'm not afraid to face Judgment. I was as good a man as I knew how to be.

[*Church bells can be heard in the distance again.*]

JIM: I used to imagine getting married when I'd lie here listening to those bells. Now I lie here and imagine . . . I don't know . . . somehow they're elegiac. They just make me sad. I know I'll never hear them with Alice lying beside me again.

Interpretation

1. What is the prevailing mood? Why do you think so?

2. What is the major difference in the way Jim and Cole accept their circumstances? Who has the more realistic outlook? What makes you think so?

3. Do you like the characters? Are they sympathetic? Why or why not? How would you want an audience to feel about them?

4. Draw a diagram of the setting you would use. How would you block the cutting?

5. Who is the more important character in this cutting? Why do you think so?

6. Do you like this cutting? Explain. How would you want an audience to feel about it?

Act 3, scene 2

Othello, the Moor of Venice

William Shakespeare

W hereas *The Two Gentlemen of Verona* deals with deceit in a humorous fashion, there is nothing at all humorous about the deceit practiced by the character Iago against Othello.

Iago has been passed over for promotion in the army in favor of the younger Cassio. He decides to take revenge against his commander, Othello, who has recently wed Desdemona.

Although deeply in love, Othello cannot help feeling insecure in the relationship. This shows up in his tendency toward jealousy. It is this weakness that Iago perceives and plays upon.

Through cunning and insinuation, he sets out to damage Desdemona's reputation. Othello falls into the trap that Iago has set, ready to believe anything that the other man tells him about her. In this cutting, set in the palace garden, Iago is busy sowing seeds of doubt in Othello's mind.

OTHELLO: Excellent wretch! Perdition catch my soul
But I do love thee! And when I love thee not,
Chaos is come again.

IAGO: My noble lord—

OTHELLO: What dost thou say, Iago?

IAGO: Did Michael Cassio, when you wooed my lady,
Know of your love?

OTHELLO: He did, from first to last. Why dost thou ask?

IAGO: But for a satisfaction of my thought,
No further harm.

OTHELLO: Why of thy thought, Iago?

IAGO: I did not think he had been acquainted with her.

OTHELLO: Oh yes, and went between us very oft.

IAGO: Indeed!

OTHELLO: Indeed! Aye, indeed. Discern'st thou aught in that?
    Is he not honest?

IAGO: Honest, my lord!

OTHELLO: Honest! Aye, honest.

IAGO: My lord, for aught I know.

OTHELLO: What dost thou think?

IAGO: Think, my lord!

OTHELLO: Think, my lord! By Heaven, he echoes me
    As if there were some monster in his thought
    Too hideous to be shown. Thou dost mean something.
    I heard thee say even now thou likedst not that
    When Cassio left my wife. What didst not like?
    And when I told thee he was of my counsel
    In my whole course of wooing, thou criedst "Indeed!"
    And didst contract and purse thy brow together
    As if thou then hadst shut up in thy brain
    Some horrible conceit.[1] If thou dost love me,
    Show me thy thought.

IAGO: My lord, you know I love you.

OTHELLO: I think thou dost,
    And for[2] I know thou'rt full of love and honesty
    And weigh'st thy words before thou givest them breath,
    Therefore these stops of thine fright me the more.
    For such things in a false disloyal knave
    Are tricks of custom, but in a man that's just
    They're close delations,[3] working from the heart,
    That passion cannot rule.

IAGO: For Michael Cassio,
    I dare be sworn I think that he is honest.

OTHELLO: I think so too.

---

[1]conceit: idea or notion   [2]for: since
[3]close delations: concealed accusations

IAGO: Men should be what they seem,
    Or those that be not, would they might seem none![4]

OTHELLO: Certain, men should be what they seem.

IAGO: Why, then I think Cassio's an honest man.

OTHELLO: Nay, yet there's more in this.
    I prithee speak to me as to thy thinkings,
    As thou dost ruminate, and give thy worst of thoughts
    The worst of words.

IAGO: Good my lord, pardon me.
    Though I am bound to every act of duty,
    I am not bound to that all slaves are free to.
    Utter my thoughts? Why, say they are vile and false,
    As where's that palace whereinto foul things
    Sometimes intrude not? Who has a breast so pure
    But some uncleanly apprehensions
    Keep leets and law days, and in session sit
    With meditations lawful?[5]

OTHELLO: Thou dost conspire against thy friend, Iago,
    If thou but think'st him wronged and makest his ear
    A stranger to thy thoughts.

IAGO: I do beseech you—
    Though I perchance am vicious in my guess,
    As, I confess, it is my nature's plague
    To spy into abuses, and oft my jealousy[6]
    Shapes faults that are not—that your wisdom yet,
    From one that so imperfectly conceits,[7]
    Would take no notice, nor build yourself a trouble
    Out of his scattering[8] and unsure observance.
    It were not for your quiet nor your good,
    Nor for my manhood, honesty, or wisdom,
    To let you know my thoughts.

OTHELLO: What dost thou mean?

IAGO: Good name in man and woman, dear my lord,
    Is the immediate[9] jewel of their souls.
    Who steals my purse steals trash—'tis something, nothing,
    'Twas mine, 'tis his, and has been slave to thousands—

[4]seem none: not seem to be honest men
[5]Who . . . lawful: who has a heart so pure that it never has foul thoughts?
[6]jealousy: suspicion   [7]conceits: imagines   [8]scattering: casual
[9]immediate: most valuable

But he that filches from me my good name
Robs me of that which not enriches him
And makes me poor indeed.

OTHELLO: By Heaven, I'll know thy thoughts.

IAGO: You cannot if my heart were in your hand,
Nor shall not whilst 'tis in my custody.

OTHELLO: Ha!

IAGO: Oh, beware, my lord, of jealousy.
It is the green-eyed monster which doth mock[10]
The meat[11] it feeds on. That cuckold lives in bliss
Who, certain of his fate, loves not his wronger.[12]
But, oh, what damnèd minutes tells he o'er
Who dotes, yet doubts, suspects, yet strongly loves!

OTHELLO: Oh, misery!

IAGO: Poor and content is rich, and rich enough,
But riches fineless[13] is as poor as winter
To him that ever fears he shall be poor.
Good Heaven, the souls of all my tribe defend
From jealousy!

OTHELLO: Why, why is this?
Think'st thou I'd make a life of jealousy,
To follow still the changes of the moon
With fresh suspicions? No, to be once in doubt
Is once to be resolved.[14] Exchange me for a goat
When I shall turn the business of my soul
To such exsufflicate and blown surmises,
Matching thy inference.[15] 'Tis not to make me jealous
To say my wife is fair, feeds well, loves company,
Is free of speech, sings, plays, and dances well.
Where virtue is, these are more virtuous.
Nor from mine own weak merits will I draw
The smallest fear or doubt of her revolt,[16]
For she had eyes, and chose me. No, Iago,

---

[10]doth mock: makes a mockery of   [11]meat: the victim
[12]That . . . wronger: the wronged husband who knows of his wife's guilt and
hates her is not tormented by jealousy   [13]fineless: limitless
[14]to . . . resolved: when I find myself in doubt, I at once seek out the truth
[15]When . . . inference: when I shall allow that which concerns me most
dearly to be influenced by such trifling suggestions as yours
[16]revolt: faithlessness

Othello
Photo courtesy of Kent State University Theatre, Kent, Ohio

I'll see before I doubt, when I doubt, prove,
And on the proof, there is no more but this—
Away at once with love or jealousy!

IAGO: I am glad of it, for now I shall have reason
To show the love and duty that I bear you

With franker spirit. Therefore, as I am bound,
Receive it from me. I speak not yet of proof.
Look to your wife. Observe her well with Cassio.
Wear your eye thus, not jealous nor secure.[17]
I would not have your free and noble nature
Out of self-bounty[18] be abused, look to 't.
I know our country disposition well.
In Venice[19] they do let Heaven see the pranks
They dare not show their husbands. Their best conscience
Is not to leave 't undone, but keep 't unknown.

OTHELLO: Dost thou say so?

IAGO: She did deceive her father, marrying you,
And when she seemed to shake and fear your looks,
She loved them most.

OTHELLO: And so she did.

IAGO: Why, go to, then.
She that so young could give out such a seeming
To seel[20] her father's eyes up close as oak—
He thought 'twas witchcraft—but I am much to blame.
I humbly do beseech you for your pardon
For too much loving you.

OTHELLO: I am bound to thee forever.

IAGO: I see this hath a little dashed your spirits.

OTHELLO: Not a jot, not a jot.

IAGO: I' faith, I fear it has.
I hope you will consider what is spoke
Comes from my love, but I do see you're moved.
I am to pray you not to strain my speech
To grosser issues[21] nor to larger reach[22]
Than to suspicion.

OTHELLO: I will not.

IAGO: Should you do so, my lord,
My speech should fall into such vile success[23]
As my thoughts aim not at. Cassio's my worthy friend.—
My lord, I see you're moved.

[17]secure: overconfident   [18]self-bounty: natural goodness
[19]Venice: noted for its loose women   [20]seel: blind
[21]grosser issues: worse conclusions   [22]larger reach: more widely, beyond
[23]success: result

OTHELLO: No, not much moved.
I do not think but Desdemona's honest.[24]

IAGO: Long live she so! And long live you to think so!

OTHELLO: And yet, how nature erring from itself—

IAGO: Aye, there's the point. As—to be bold with you—
Not to affect[25] many proposed matches[26]
Of her own clime, complexion, and degree,
Whereto we see in all things nature tends[27]—
Foh! One may smell in such a will most rank,[28]
Foul disproportion, thoughts unnatural.
But pardon me. I do not in position
Distinctly speak of her, though I may fear
Her will, recoiling to her better judgment,
May fall to match[29] you with her country forms,
And happily[30] repent.

OTHELLO: Farewell, farewell.
If more thou dost perceive, let me know more.
Set on thy wife to observe. Leave me, Iago.

IAGO [*Going.*]: My lord, I take my leave.

OTHELLO: Why did I marry? This honest creature doubtless
Sees and knows more, much more, than he unfolds.

IAGO [*Returning.*]: My lord, I would I might entreat your honor
To scan this thing no further. Leave it to time.
Though it be fit that Cassio have his place,
For sure he fills it up with great ability,
Yet if you please to hold him off awhile,
You shall by that perceive him and his means.
Note if your lady strain his entertainment[31]
With any strong or vehement importunity—
Much will be seen in that. In the meantime,
Let me be thought too busy in my fears—
As worthy cause I have to fear I am—
And hold her free, I do beseech your Honor.

OTHELLO: Fear not my government.[32]

IAGO: I once more take my leave. [*Exit.*]

---

[24]honest: chaste   [25]affect: be inclined to   [26]proposed matches: offers of
marriage   [27]in . . . tends: a woman naturally marries a man of her own
country, color, and rank   [28]will . . . rank: most lustful desire
[29]match: compare   [30]happily: by chance   [31]strain . . . entertainment: urge
you to receive him   [32]government: self-control

OTHELLO: This fellow's of exceeding honesty,
And knows all qualities,[33] with a learned spirit,
Of human dealings.[34] If I do prove her haggard,
Though that her jesses were my dear heartstrings,
I'd whistle her off and let her down the wind
To prey at fortune.[35] Haply, for I am black
And have not those soft parts of conversation
That chamberers[36] have, or for I am declined
Into the vale of years—yet that's not much—
She's gone, I am abused, and my relief
Must be to loathe her. Oh, curse of marriage,
That we can call these delicate creatures ours,
And not their appetites! I had rather be a toad
And live upon the vapor of a dungeon
Than keep a corner in the thing I love
For others' uses. Yet, 'tis the plague of great ones,
Prerogatived[37] are they less than the base.
'Tis destiny unshunnable, like death.
Even then this forkèd plague[38] is fated to us
When we do quicken.[39]

[33]qualities: different kinds
[34]with . . . dealings: with wide experience of human nature
[35]If . . . fortune: if she's wild, let her go because she's not worth keeping
[36]chamberers: playboys   [37]Prerogatived: privileged
[38]forked plague: to be a cuckold   [39]quicken: move inside the womb

Interpretation

1. Do you like Othello? Iago? Why or why not?

2. Is the action believable? Explain.

3. What provides the conflict in this cutting? Why do you think so?

4. How would you stage this as far as movement? Setting? Costuming?

5. Othello is black, Desdemona white. Do you think this has any influence on Othello's feelings about the relationship? On Iago's? Why or why not?

6. Pick out the "plot lines," those that advance the story. How would you try to make sure the audience grasps and understands them?

Act 1

A Thousand Clowns

Herb Gardner

Years ago, Nick's mother walked out for a pack of cigarettes, leaving him in the care of his Uncle Murray. She returned six years later for her luggage, only to leave again. Consequently, Murray has reared Nick, allowing him a great amount of freedom, even to deciding on what to call himself.

They have a good relationship. The problem is that Murray was a writer for a children's television show, featuring Chuckles the Chipmunk. When he could no longer stand the job, he quit. Now he is being investigated by the Child Welfare Board to see if he is maintaining a proper home atmosphere for his nephew.

The action occurs in Murray's one-room apartment, which is comfortable-looking but cluttered with all sorts of junk.

MURRAY [*Walking across to the bed.*] Get those kids outa here. [*Sits on the bed.*] Nick, what'd I tell you about bringing your friends in here this early in the morning?

NICK: It's not my friends; it's the T.V.

MURRAY: Play with your friends outside. Get those kids out of here. [NICK *turns the set off.* MURRAY *looks over at the front door, waves at it and shouts.*] Good. And none of you kids come back here till this afternoon.

NICK: It wasn't my friends. It was Chuckles the Chipmunk.

MURRAY [*Sleepily.*]: That's very comforting.

NICK [*Brings a pack of cigarettes to* MURRAY.]: Boy it's a terrible program now. It was a much better show when you were writing it.

MURRAY: When Sandburg and Faulkner quit, I quit. What kind of a day is it outside?

NICK [*Going to the kitchen.*]: It's a Monday.

MURRAY: I mean warm or cold or sunny is what I mean.

NICK: I haven't been outside yet.

MURRAY [*He pulls the blind up revealing the windows; there is no change whatever in the lighting, the room remains dark. The windows have no view other than the gray blank wall of the building a few feet opposite.*]: Ah, light. [*He leans out of the window, cranes his head around to look up at the sky.*] Can't see a thing. Not a thing. [*Pulls his head back in.*] No matter what time of day or what season, we got a permanent fixture out there; twilight in February.

NICK [*Bringing the coffee pot out of the kitchen and filling MURRAY'S cup.*]: You better call the weather record like always.

MURRAY: One morning I'll wake up and that damn building'll have fallen down into Seventh Avenue so I can see the weather. [*Picks up the phone; dialing.*] Using a machine to call up another machine. I do not enjoy the company of ghosts. [*Into the phone.*] Hello, Weather Lady! Well, I'm just fine, and how is your nasal little self this morning? What's the weather? Uh-huh. That high? And the wind, which way does the wind blow this morning? Ah, good. Uh-huh, all the way to East Point and Block Island. Humidity? Very decent. Whoops, oh, there you go again. You simply *must* learn not to repeat yourself. I keep telling you every morning that once is enough. You'll never learn. [*Hangs up.*] Women seldom sense when they have become boring. [*Goes to the window again, leans out, raises his voice, shouting out of the window.*] Neighbors, I have an announcement for you. I have *never seen* such a collection of dirty windows. Now I want to see you all out there on the fire escape with your Mr. Clean bottles, and let's snap it up . . .

NICK: Gee, Murray, you gotta shout like that every morning?

MURRAY: It clears my head. [*After glancing around clock-filled apartment.*] What time is it?

NICK: It's eight-forty.

MURRAY: Well, what're you doing here? Why aren't you in school?

NICK: It's a holiday. It's Irving R. Feldman's birthday, like you said.

MURRAY: Irving R. Feldman's birthday is my own personal national holiday. I did not open it up for the public. He is proprietor of perhaps the most distinguished kosher delicatessen in this neighborhood and as such I hold the day of his birth in reverence.

NICK: You said you weren't going to look for work today because it was Irving R. Feldman's birthday, so I figured I would celebrate too, a little.

MURRAY: Don't kid *me*, Nick, you know you're supposed to be in school. I thought you *liked* that damn genius' school—why the hell—

NICK: Well, I figured I'd better stay home today till you got up. [*Hesitantly.*] There's something I gotta discuss with you. See, because it's this special school for big brains they watch you and take notes and make reports and smile at you a lot. And there's this psychologist who talks to you every week, each kid separately. He's the biggest smiler they got up there.

MURRAY: Because you got brains they figure you're nuts.

NICK: Anyway, we had Show and Tell time in Mrs. Zimmerman's class on Monday; and each kid in the class is supposed to tell about some trip he took and show pictures. Well, y'remember when I made you take me with you to the El Bambino Club over on Fifty-second?

MURRAY: Nick . . . you showed and you told.

NICK: Well, it turned out they're very square up at the Revere School. And sometimes in class, when we have our Wednesday Free-Association-Talk Period, I sometimes quote you on different opinions . . .

MURRAY: That wasn't a good idea.

NICK: Well, I didn't know they were such nervous people there. Murray, they're very nervous there. And then there was this composition I wrote in Creative Writing about the advantages of Unemployment Insurance.

MURRAY: Why did you write about that?

NICK: It was just on my mind. Then once they got my record out they started to notice what they call "significant data." Turns out they've been keeping this file on me for a long time, and checking with that Child Welfare place; same place you got those letters from.

MURRAY: I never answer letters from large organizations.

NICK: So, Murray . . . when they come over here, I figure we'd better . . .

MURRAY: When they come over here?

NICK: Yeah, this Child Welfare crowd, they want to take a look at our environment here.

MURRAY: Oh, that's charming. Why didn't you tell me about this before, Nick?

NICK: Well, y'know, the past coupla nights we couldn't get together.

MURRAY: That was unavoidable. You know when I have a lot of work you stay up at Mrs. Myers'.

NICK [Pointing at the dresser.]: Murray; your work forgot her gloves last night.

MURRAY: That's very bright.

NICK: Anyway, for this Child Welfare crowd, I figure we better set up some kind of story before they get here.

MURRAY: You make it sound like a vice raid.

NICK: I mean, for one thing, you don't even have a job right now.

MURRAY: Look, you want me to put up some kind of front when they get here? O.K., I will. Don't worry, kid. I'll snow 'em good.

NICK: I thought maybe you could at least look in the papers for a job, this morning before they get here. So we could tell them about your possibilities.

MURRAY [Without much conviction.]: I look every day.

NICK: Couldn't I just read you from the Times again like last week? While you get dressed?

MURRAY: O.K., read me from the paper. [He starts to get dressed.]

NICK: And then, maybe, you'll take a shave?

MURRAY: All right, all right.

NICK [Picking up the Times from the swivel chair.]: This paper is three days old.

MURRAY: So what do you want me to do, bury it? Is it starting to rot or something? Read me from the paper.

NICK: But most of these jobs, somebody must have taken them. Look, I'll go down and get a newer—

MURRAY: We do *not* need a newer paper. All the really important jobs stay forever. Now start on the first page of Help-Wanted-Male and read me from the paper.

NICK: O.K. [*Puts on his glasses; reads aloud.*] "Administ, Exoppty. To ninety dollars." What's that?

MURRAY: Administrative Assistant, excellent opportunity. Nothing. Keep reading.

NICK: But ninety dollars would be ninety dollars more than nothing. Nothing is what you make now.

MURRAY: Have you ever considered being the first twelve-year-old boy in space?

NICK: But, ninety dollars . . .

MURRAY: *You* go be an Administ, Exoppty. They *need* men like you. Read further.

NICK [*Reading from the paper.*]: "Versatile Junior, traffic manager, industrial representative organization. One hundred to one hundred twenty-five dollars. Call Mr. Shiffman."

MURRAY [*Picks up the cardboard from his shirt collar and talks into it.*]: Hello, Mr. Shiffman? I read your name in the New York *Times,* so I know you must be real. My name is Mandrake the Magician. I am a versatile Junior and I would like to manage your traffic for you. You see, sir, it has long been my ambition to work in a pointless job, with no future and a cretin like you as my boss . . .

NICK: But Murray, it says "one hundred twenty-five dollars," that's a lot of . . .

MURRAY: Just read the ads. No editorial comment or personal recommendations. When I need your advice, I'll ask for it. Out of the mouths of babes comes drooling.

NICK: You said that last week. Murray, you don't want a job is the whole thing.

MURRAY: Would you just concentrate on being a child? Because I find your imitation of an adult hopelessly inadequate.

NICK: You want to be your own boss, but the trouble with that is you don't pay yourself anything. [NICK *decides that what he has just said is very funny. He laughs.*] Hey—you don't pay yourself anything—that's a good line—I gotta remember that.

MURRAY: That's what *you* said last week.

NICK: Look, Murray. [*He puts the paper down and stands up.*] Can I speak to you man to man?

MURRAY: That was cute about a year ago, buddy, but that line has got to go.

NICK [*Takes off his glasses.*]: Murray, I am upset. For me as an actual child the way you live in this house and we live is a dangerous thing for my later life when I become an actual person. An unemployed person like you are for so many months is bad for you as the person involved and is definitely bad for me who he lives with in the same house where the rent isn't paid for months sometimes. And I wish you would get a job, Murray. Please.

Interpretation

1. What is the central idea of this cutting? What provides the major conflict? The secondary conflict?

2. Do you like Nick and Murray? Why or why not? What about them would you want to convey to an audience?

3. Why do you think Nick "showed and told" the things he did at school? Was it realistic or not that he would do this?

4. How do Nick and Murray feel about each other? How do you know?

5. What is the dominant mood of this cutting?

6. What are the most important traits of Murray and Nick that you'd want an audience to grasp in this cutting? How would you try to convey them?

7. How would you portray the increasing tension in the cutting?

Two Gentlemen of Verona

William Shakespeare

The two gentlemen are Valentine and Proteus, two devoted friends. Valentine is leaving for the Emperor's court in Milan, while Proteus is staying at home, seeking to woo Julia, who, unbeknownst to him, has many suitors. At the same time Proteus' father, believing that his son should have a chance to travel, decides to send him after Valentine. This is how the first act ends.

This cutting is the beginning of the second act. Speed, the second character in this scene, is Valentine's servant.

SCENE 1. *Milan. The* DUKE'S *palace.*

[*Enter* VALENTINE *and* SPEED.]

SPEED: Sir, your glove.

VALENTINE: Not mine. My gloves are on.

SPEED: Why, then, this may be yours, for this is but one.

VALENTINE: Ha! Let me see. Aye, give it me, it's mine.
  Sweet ornament that decks a thing divine!
  Ah, Silvia, Silvia!

SPEED: Madam Silvia! Madam Silvia!

VALENTINE: How now, sirrah?[1]

SPEED: She is not within hearing, sir.

VALENTINE: Why, sir, who bade you call her?

[1]sirrah: term of address used to an inferior

SPEED: Your Worship, sir, or else I mistook.

VALENTINE: Well, you'll still[2] be too forward.

SPEED: And yet I was last chidden for being too slow.

VALENTINE: Go to,[3] sir. Tell me, do you know Madam Silvia?

SPEED: She that your Worship loves?

VALENTINE: Why, how know you that I am in love?

SPEED: Marry,[4] by these special marks. First, you have learned, like Sir Proteus, to wreathe[5] your arms like a malecontent, to relish a love song like a robin redbreast, to walk alone like one that had the pestilence, to sigh like a schoolboy that had lost his A B C,[6] to weep like a young wench that had buried her grandam,[7] to fast like one that takes diet, to watch like one that fears robbing, to speak puling like a beggar at Hallowmas.[8] You were wont, when you laughed, to crow like a cock; when you walked, to walk like one of the lions; when you fasted, it was presently[9] after dinner; when you looked sadly, it was for want of money; and now you are metamorphosed with a mistress, that, when I look on you, I can hardly think you my master.

VALENTINE: Are all these things perceived in me?

SPEED: They are all perceived without ye.

VALENTINE: Without me? They cannot.

SPEED: Without you? Nay, that's certain, for without[10] you were so simple, none else would; but you are so without these follies that these follies are within you, and shine through you like the water in an urinal,[11] that not an eye that sees you but is a physician to comment on your malady.

VALENTINE: But tell me, dost thou know my lady Silvia?

SPEED: She that you gaze on so as she sits at supper?

[2]still: always   [3]Go to: exclamation of impatience
[4]Marry: by the Virgin Mary
[5]wreathe . . . Hallowmas: Speed lists the signs of a melancholy lover
[6]A B C: a school book used for learning to read   [7]grandam: grandmother
[8]Hallowmas: All Saints' Day, November 1, when it was the custom to beg for alms in return for praying for the soul of the giver's friends
[9]presently: immediately   [10]without: unless
[11]water . . . urinal: inspection of urine was a way of diagnosing an illness, used by reputable physicians and quacks alike

VALENTINE: Hast thou observed that? Even she, I mean.

SPEED: Why, sir, I know her not.

VALENTINE: Dost thou know her by my gazing on her, and yet knowest her not?

SPEED: Is she not hard-favored,[12] sir?

VALENTINE: Not so fair, boy, as well-favored.[13]

SPEED: Sir, I know that well enough.

VALENTINE: What dost thou know?

SPEED: That she is not so fair as, of you, well-favored.

VALENTINE: I mean that her beauty is exquisite, but her favor infinite.

SPEED: That's because the one is painted, and the other out of all count.[14]

VALENTINE: How painted? And how out of count?

SPEED: Marry, sir, so painted, to make her fair, that no man counts on her beauty.

VALENTINE: How esteemest thou me? I account of her beauty.

SPEED: You never saw her since she was deformed.[15]

VALENTINE: How long hath she been deformed?

SPEED: Ever since you loved her.

VALENTINE: I have loved her ever since I saw her, and still I see her beautiful.

SPEED: If you love her, you cannot see her.

VALENTINE: Why?

SPEED: Because Love is blind. Oh, that you had mine eyes, or your own eyes had the lights they were wont to have when you chid at Sir Proteus for going ungartered!

VALENTINE: What should I see then?

[12]hard-favored: homely
[13]well-favored: good looking, with puns on "favored" meaning liked and "favor" meaning kindness. Speed interprets the word to mean *face*.
[14]one . . . count: her face (the one) is made up (painted) and her beauty (the other) cannot be reckoned (out of count).
[15]deformed: transformed by love

SPEED: Your own present folly, and her passing[16] deformity; for he, being in love, could not see to garter his hose, and you, being in love, cannot see to put on your hose.

VALENTINE: Belike, boy, then, you are in love, for last morning you could not see to wipe my shoes.

SPEED: True, sir, I was in love with my bed. I thank you, you swinged[17] me for my love, which makes me the bolder to chide you for yours.

VALENTINE: In conclusion, I stand affected to her.

SPEED: I would you were set,[18] so your affection would cease.

VALENTINE: Last night she enjoined me to write some lines to one she loves.

SPEED: And have you?

VALENTINE: I have.

SPEED: Are they not lamely writ?

VALENTINE: No, boy, but as well as I can do them. Peace! Here she comes.

[16]passing: exceeding
[17]swinged: beat
[18]set: seated, as a contrast to stand in the preceding line

Interpretation

1. What is the purpose of this cutting?

2. What type of setting would you use? What type of costumes? Why?

3. What can you tell about the characters of the two men?

4. What in this cutting is most important for an audience to know?

5. Is the dialogue realistic or not? Justify your answer.

Act 1, scene 1

The Way of the World

William Congreve

This play deals with deceit among the upper-class English. The intricate plot involves the wooing of Millamant by Mirabell and the compromise that results. Much of the humor and delight derives from the fact that the two lovers know the "way of the world," and are not duped into sentimentality.

The cutting opens the play.

SCENE: *London*
   The time equal to that of the representation.
   A chocolate-house.

[MIRABELL *and* FAINALL *rising from cards.* BETTY *waiting.*]

MIRABELL: You are a fortunate man, Mr. Fainall!

FAINALL: Have we done?

MIRABELL: What you please: I'll play on to entertain you.

FAINALL: No, I'll give you your revenge another time, when you are not so indifferent; you are thinking of something else now, and play too negligently; the coldness of a losing gamester lessens the pleasure of the winner. I'd no more play with a man that slighted his ill fortune than I'd make love to a woman who undervalued the loss of her reputation.

MIRABELL: You have a taste extremely delicate, and are for refining on your pleasures.

FAINALL: Prithee, why so reserved? Something has put you out of humor.

MIRABELL: Not at all: I happen to be grave to-day, and you are gay; that's all.

FAINALL: Confess, Millamant and you quarreled last night after I left you; my fair cousin has some humors that would tempt the patience of a Stoic. What, some coxcomb came in, and was well received by her, while you were by?

MIRABELL: Witwoud and Petulant; and what was worse, her aunt, your wife's mother, my evil genius; or to sum up all in her own name, my old Lady Wishfort came in.

FAINALL: Oh, there it is then! She has a lasting passion for you, and with reason.—What, then my wife was there?

MIRABELL: Yes, and Mrs. Marwood, and three or four more, whom I never saw before. Seeing me, they all put on their grave faces, whispered to one another; then complained aloud of the vapors, and after fell into a profound silence.

FAINALL: They had a mind to be rid of you.

MIRABELL: For which reason I resolved not to stir. At last the good old lady broke through her painful taciturnity with an invective against long visits. I would not have understood her, but Millamant joining in the argument, I rose, and, with a constrained smile, told her I thought nothing was so easy as to know when a visit began to be troublesome. She reddened, and I withdrew, without expecting her reply.

FAINALL: You were to blame to resent what she spoke only in compliance with her aunt.

MIRABELL: She is more mistress of herself than to be under the necessity of such a resignation.

FAINALL: What! though half her fortune depends upon her marrying with my lady's approbation?

MIRABELL: I was then in such a humor, that I should have been better pleased if she had been less discreet.

FAINALL: Now, I remember, I wonder not they were weary of you; last night was one of their cabal nights; they have 'em three times a-week, and meet by turns at one another's apartments, where they come together like the coroner's inquest, to sit upon the murdered reputations of the week. You and I are excluded; and it was once proposed that all the male sex should be excepted; but somebody moved that, to avoid scandal, there might be one man of the community; upon which motion Witwoud and Petulant were enrolled members.

MIRABELL: And who may have been the foundress of this sect? My Lady Wishfort, I warrant, who publishes her detestation of mankind; and full of the vigor of fifty-five, declares for a friend and ratafia; and let posterity shift for itself, she'll breed no more.

FAINALL: The discovery of your sham addresses to her, to conceal your love to her niece, has provoked this separation; had you dissembled better, things might have continued in the state of nature.

MIRABELL: I did as much as man could, with any reasonable conscience; I proceeded to the very last act of flattery with her, and was guilty of a song in her commendation. Nay, I got a friend to put her into a lampoon and compliment her with the imputation of an affair with a young fellow, which I carried so far, that I told her the malicious town took notice that she was grown fat of a sudden; and when she lay in of a dropsy, persuaded her she was reported to be in labor. The devil's in't, if an old woman is to be flattered further, unless a man should endeavor downright personally to debauch her; and that my virtue forbade me. But for the discovery of this amour I am indebted to your friend, or your wife's friend, Mrs. Marwood.

FAINALL: What should provoke her to be your enemy, unless she has made you advances which you have slighted? Women do not easily forgive omissions of that nature.

MIRABELL: She was always civil to me till of late.—I confess I am not one of those coxcombs who are apt to interpret a woman's good manners to her prejudice, and think that she who does not refuse 'em everything, can refuse 'em nothing.

FAINALL: You are a gallant man, Mirabell; and though you may have cruelty enough not to satisfy a lady's longing, you have too much generosity not to be tender of her honor. Yet you speak with an indifference which seems to be affected, and confesses you are conscious of a negligence.

MIRABELL: You pursue the argument with a distrust that seems to be unaffected, and confesses you are conscious of a concern for which the lady is more indebted to you than is your wife.

FAINALL: Fie, fie, friend! if you grow censorious I must leave you.— I'll look upon the gamesters in the next room.

Interpretation

1. What is the purpose of this cutting?

2. What type of setting would you use? What type of costumes? Why?

3. What can you tell about the characters of the two men?

4. What is the most important thing the audience should know about this cutting?

5. Is the dialogue realistic? Justify your answer.

CUTTINGS FOR ONE MAN AND ONE WOMAN

A Thing of Beauty

The Taming of the Shrew

Arms and the Man

The Tattoo Parlor

Fashion

Cyrano de Bergerac

Arms and the Man
Photo courtesy of Kent State
University Theatre, Kent, Ohio

A Thing of Beauty

Charles Kray

I t is the late 1930s; the Nazis are in power in Germany, seeking to deal with the "Jewish problem." The Jews, they feel, represent a threat to society and should be purged or put to death.

The Colonel is a Nazi. He is searching for Edith Stein, a Jewish woman whom he believes has been given asylum at a convent. The convent is familiar to him from his school days, when the prioress was his teacher.

Nineteen nuns are being held hostage. The Colonel threatens that they will be killed one by one until Edith Stein is discovered. He further states that he suspects that one of the nuns, Sister Benedicta, actually is Edith Stein. He has asked to see her. The scene is the receiving room of a convent in Germany.

BENEDICTA: Why are you here, Colonel?

COLONEL: I was looking for someone. But now I want to prove something to myself.

BENEDICTA: What, Colonel?

COLONEL: In due time, Sister. Meanwhile I will ask the questions.

BENEDICTA: As you wish.

COLONEL: Tell me, Sister. How do you feel about the Catholic religion?

BENEDICTA: That seems a strange question.

COLONEL: I suppose. But in my field I sometimes get the clearest answers from strange questions.

BENEDICTA: Just what is your field, Colonel?

COLONEL: I'm an intelligence officer, Sister.

BENEDICTA: That sounds rather ostentatious.

COLONEL: Not really, Sister. Intelligence indicates a branch of service, not a man's description.

BENEDICTA: I see.

COLONEL: Now would you mind answering my strange question?

BENEDICTA: How I feel about the Catholic religion?

COLONEL: Yes.

BENEDICTA: I embrace it.

COLONEL: Is that all?

BENEDICTA: I embrace it with every fibre of my being. With my entire capacity to love. It is my solace, my joy, my comfort. It is my life.

COLONEL: Is this a required attitude for a Carmelite or your own personal conception?

BENEDICTA: My own. My feeling.

COLONEL: Feeling? Is this the Carmelite feeling?

BENEDICTA: Perhaps.

COLONEL: Then it is a required attitude.

BENEDICTA: No. Only duties are required. An attitude is developed.

COLONEL: I see. Sister, how long have you been a Carmelite?

BENEDICTA: A year.

COLONEL: Only a year? That seems odd.

BENEDICTA: Odd?

COLONEL: Well, I wouldn't classify you as a young nun.

BENEDICTA: I was a postulant for some time before that.

COLONEL: A postulant?

BENEDICTA: A novice preparing to take the vows.

COLONEL: Is that like medical internship . . . taking seven or eight years?

BENEDICTA: No, Colonel.

COLONEL: How long, then?

BENEDICTA: It depends upon the individual. The time can vary from six months to two years.

COLONEL: And how long were you a . . . posturer, is it?

BENEDICTA: Postulant, Colonel.

COLONEL: Yes, postulant. How long were you a postulant?

BENEDICTA: Six months.

COLONEL: Would you mind telling me your age, Sister?

BENEDICTA: Not at all, Colonel. I am 40.

COLONEL: And you have been a nun for one year only? What was the reason for the delay? Why didn't you become a nun sooner?

BENEDICTA: I was a teacher and my superiors felt I was needed more in the schools.

COLONEL: What about as a young girl? Did you, how do you Catholics put it, receive the call then?

BENEDICTA: No, I did not.

COLONEL: When did you receive it?

BENEDICTA: Colonel, is all this information necessary?

COLONEL: I'm afraid it is. When did you receive the call?

BENEDICTA: About five years ago.

COLONEL: Wasn't that rather late?

BENEDICTA: Not for me.

COLONEL: I don't understand.

BENEDICTA: I became a Catholic six years ago.

COLONEL: Really! This becomes more and more interesting. What were you before?

BENEDICTA: I followed the philosophy of Edmund Husserl.

COLONEL: Husserl? Germany's soap-box phenomenologist. I'm surprised. I thought he was for immature college freshmen.

BENEDICTA: Perhaps. Perhaps you are not far wrong in that description, Colonel. Perhaps he opens the doors of learning for immature college freshmen.

COLONEL: And did his philosophy open any doors for you?

BENEDICTA: To study any philosophy is to walk on the edge of an abyss.

COLONEL: And you fell into the abyss of Catholicism.

BENEDICTA: Colonel, you have a distinct gift for shading a statement of fact to make it fit your own conclusions.

COLONEL: An old trick of my trade, Sister. Never allow the enemy the indulgence of accepting a positive statement.

BENEDICTA: Am I your enemy, Colonel?

COLONEL: I don't know, Sister. I hope to find out.

BENEDICTA: Then I am guilty until proven innocent?

COLONEL: Guilty? of what, Sister?

BENEDICTA: I don't know, Colonel, *I* hope to find out.

[*They both laugh.*]

COLONEL: Very good, Sister. You've won the point, but I've won my bet.

BENEDICTA: Bet, Colonel?

COLONEL: Yes. You know Field Major Wollman, your military governor?

BENEDICTA: Only by sight. He has been here visiting.

COLONEL: Well, he knows you. When he found I was coming here, he said "Watch that Benedicta, the brooding one, she never smiles."

BENEDICTA: He wasn't very gallant.

COLONEL: I defended you, Sister. I defended womankind. I said there wasn't a woman alive who never smiles. So we bet on it.

BENEDICTA: And you won.

COLONEL: Didn't I?

BENEDICTA: Colonel, I find you most amazing. You are a high officer investigating our convent for some seemingly important reason and you spend the time making small talk. I find it most pleasant, but I'm sure we both have more important things to do.

COLONEL: You never let your guard down for a moment, do you Sister?

[*She doesn't answer.*]

Very well. Sister, phenomenology is not a common religion handed down from parent to child. Were you always an advocate of Husserl?

BENEDICTA: Before I studied Edmund Husserl's philosophy I was an atheist.

COLONEL: Were your parents atheists?

BENEDICTA: I was an orphan. Colonel, I am aware that you have a file of biographical material concerning me. Are you trying to get me to make a mistake and give you information which differs from that in my file?

COLONEL: No, Sister. As a matter of fact, the reason for my questioning is for the lack of information in your file. There seems to be very little of anything concerning your life prior to your entering this convent. This is quite unusual. Of course all the information you give me will be checked. Therefore, I should caution you to be accurate as well as truthful. [*He reads from file.*] You were an orphan in the town of Augsburg, raised by Grandparents who are now deceased. Other school records were destroyed in a fire in that community some ten years ago. If you were a criminal, that would be a very convenient set of circumstances.

BENEDICTA: My background was checked by the papal authorities when I became a nun.

COLONEL: And very well, I should imagine. I understand their Gestapo is as effective as ours.

BENEDICTA: Colonel, I find your sense of humor lacking in both sense and humor.

COLONEL: I'm sorry, Sister. But I can't resist the temptation of poking at something seemingly so impregnable and formidable as the Catholic religion.

BENEDICTA: Why don't you try Naziism?

COLONEL: Believe me, Sister, I have. I don't know why I said that. I suppose it's because I know that if this room had a microphone in it, I would have been the one to put it there. But you're much too sensitive, Sister. You find my sense of humor lacking. I find you lacking a sense of humor.

BENEDICTA: Colonel, what started as an interrogation, has seemingly turned into a social visit. Are you trying to be disarming, Colonel?

COLONEL: Not at all, Sister. Not at all. Sister, you make me feel like a recalcitrant student. I haven't felt like that in years, and I'm enjoying the feeling. If I weren't, Sister, I could have you thrown in jail just for the disdain in your voice when you speak of the German state.

BENEDICTA: Should I be thankful, Colonel?

COLONEL: No, Sister. In a sense, I should be. It's refreshing.

[*Pause.*]

Sister, before you became an atheist, what religion did you *embrace?* [*He smiles.*]

BENEDICTA: Colonel, I find your choice of words as wanting as your sense of humor.

[*He laughs.*]

My grandfather was a man of the earth. He believed in a God, but this God communicated with my grandfather through the soil. The wonder of this phenomena was religion enough for my grandfather so we did not belong to any formal religion.

COLONEL: I should think such a simple philosophy would have impressed you. Yet you seem to have flitted from one religion to another until at a very late age you became imbued with the Catholic faith and after this incomprehensible conversion, you commit an even more astounding act by taking the vows of a Carmelite nun at the very late age of 40.

Interpretation

1. What is the central idea of this cutting?

2. How does the Colonel feel about Sister Benedicta? How does she feel about him?

3. Which lines are the most important? How would you emphasize them for an audience?

4. What are the dominant traits of the characters? The secondary traits?

5. What is the prevailing mood of this cutting? What sort of atmosphere would you want to create for the audience? Why?

6. Do you think the "given circumstances" and the situation are realistic? Why or why not?

Act 2, scene 1

The Taminq of the Shrew

William Shakespeare

In this play within a play, a tinker is found drunk, then dressed in rich clothes and, when awakened, told he has recovered from an insanity that has lasted fifteen years. In order to keep him sane, a company of traveling actors performs *The Taming of the Shrew* for him.

The plot deals with the wooing of two daughters, Katharina, the eldest, whose "only fault . . . is that she is intolerably curst and shrewd and forward," and Bianca, her younger sister, "as modest and gentle as Katharina is wild and unruly." Their father decrees that Katharina must marry before Bianca can. One of Bianca's suitors finds an old friend, Petruchio, and persuades him to woo Katharina. The cutting is set in the house of Katharina and Bianca's father.

[*Enter* KATHARINA.]

PETRUCHIO: Good morrow, Kate; for that's your name, I hear.

KATHARINA: Well have you heard, but something hard of hearing.
    They call me Katharine[1] that do talk of me.

PETRUCHIO: You lie, in faith, for you are called plain Kate,
    And bonny Kate, and sometimes Kate the Curst;
    But Kate, the prettiest Kate in Christendom,
    Kate of Kate-Hall, my superdainty Kate,
    For dainties are all Kates[2]—and therefore, Kate,
    Take this of me, Kate of my consolation:
    Hearing thy mildness praised in every town,

[1]Petruchio is being rude by calling her Kate without her permission to do so
[2]dainties . . . Kates: a pun on "cate" or deli*cate*

Thy virtues spoke of, and thy beauty sounded,
Yet not so deeply as to thee belongs,
Myself am moved to woo thee for my wife.

KATHARINA: Moved! In good time. Let him that moved you hither
Remove you hence. I knew you at the first
You were a movable.[3]

PETRUCHIO: Why, what's a movable?

KATHARINA: A joined stool.[4]

PETRUCHIO: Thou hast hit it. Come sit on me.

KATHARINA: Asses are made to bear, and so are you.

PETRUCHIO: Women are made to bear, and so are you.

KATHARINA: No such jade as you, if me you mean.

PETRUCHIO: Alas, good Kate, I will not burden thee!
For, knowing thee to be but young and light—

KATHARINA: Too light for such a swain[5] as you to catch,
And yet as heavy as my weight should be.

PETRUCHIO: Should be! Should—buzz![6]

KATHARINA: Well ta'en, and like a buzzard.[7]

PETRUCHIO: O slow-winged turtle! Shall a buzzard take thee?

KATHARINA: Aye, for a turtle, as he takes a buzzard.[8]

PETRUCHIO: Come, come, you wasp. I' faith, you are too angry.

KATHARINA: If I be waspish, best beware my sting.

PETRUCHIO: My remedy is then to pluck it out.

KATHARINA: Aye, if the fool could find it where it lies.

PETRUCHIO: Who knows not where a wasp does wear his sting?
In his tail.

KATHARINA: In his tongue.

PETRUCHIO: Whose tongue?

---

[3]movable: piece of furniture
[4]joined stool: a type of four-legged, rectangular stool
[5]swain: country lover   [6]buzz: with a pun on *be*
[7]buzzard: a fool, or a hawk unsuitable for hawking
[8]Aye . . . buzzard: I'm as unlikely to choose you as a turtledove to mate with a buzzard

KATHARINA: Yours, if you talk of tails; and so farewell.

PETRUCHIO: What, with my tongue in your tail? Nay, come again.
Good Kate, I am a gentleman.

KATHARINA: That I'll try.[9] [*She strikes him.*]

PETRUCHIO: I swear I'll cuff you if you strike again.

KATHARINA: So may you lose your arms.
If you strike me, you are no gentleman,
And if no gentleman, why then no arms.

PETRUCHIO: A herald, Kate? Oh, put me in thy books![10]

KATHARINA: What is your crest? A coxcomb?

PETRUCHIO: A combless cock, so Kate will be my hen.

KATHARINA: No cock of mine. You crow too like a craven.[11]

PETRUCHIO: Nay, come, Kate, come. You must not look so sour.

KATHARINA: It is my fashion when I see a crab.[12]

PETRUCHIO: Why, here's no crab, and therefore look not sour.

KATHARINA: There is, there is.

PETRUCHIO: Then show it me.

KATHARINA: Had I a glass, I would.

PETRUCHIO: What, you mean my face?

KATHARINA: Well aimed of such a young[13] one.

PETRUCHIO: Now, by Saint George, I am too young for you.

KATHARINA: Yet you are withered.

PETRUCHIO: 'Tis with cares.

KATHARINA: I care not.

PETRUCHIO: Nay, hear you, Kate. In sooth you scape not so.

KATHARINA: I chafe you if I tarry. Let me go.

[9]That . . . try: if he is a gentleman, he will not strike back
[10]herald . . . books: put me in your *Social Register*
[11]craven: a gamecock that will not fight
[12]crab: crab apple
[13]young: inexperienced; one line later *young* means *agile*

The Taming of the Shrew
Photo courtesy of Kent State University Theatre, Kent, Ohio

PETRUCHIO: No, not a whit. I find you passing gentle.
'Twas told me you were rough and coy and sullen,
And now I find report a very liar;
For thou art pleasant, gamesome, passing courteous,
But slow in speech, yet sweet as springtime flowers.
Thou canst not frown, thou canst not look askance,[14]
Nor bite the lip, as angry wenches will,
Nor hast thou pleasure to be cross in talk,
But thou with mildness entertain'st thy wooers,
With gentle conference, soft and affable.
Why does the world report that Kate doth limp?[15]
O slanderous world! Kate like the hazel twig
Is straight and slender, and as brown in hue
As hazel nuts, and sweeter than the kernels.
Oh, let me see thee walk. Thou dost not halt.[16]

KATHARINA: Go, fool, and whom thou keep'st command.

PETRUCHIO: Did ever Dian[17] so become a grove
As Kate this chamber with her princely gait?
Oh, be thou Dian, and let her be Kate,
And then let Kate be chaste and Dian sportful!

KATHARINA: Where did you study all this goodly speech?

PETRUCHIO: It is extempore, from my mother wit.

KATHARINA: A witty mother! Witless else[19] her son.

PETRUCHIO: Am I not wise?

KATHARINA: Yes. Keep you warm.[19]

PETRUCHIO: Marry, so I mean, sweet Katharine, in thy bed,
And therefore, setting all this chat aside,
Thus in plain terms: Your father has consented
That you shall be my wife, your dowry 'greed on,
And, will you, nill you,[20] I will marry you.
Now Kate, I am a husband for your turn.
For, by this light whereby I see thy beauty,
Thy beauty, that doth make me like thee well,

[14]askance: scornfully
[15]doth limp: is deformed
[16]halt: limp
[17]Dian: Diana, goddess of chastity and of the hunt or chase
[18]Witless else: if your mother had not been witty, you would have been a fool
[19]Keep warm: refers to the proverb, "He has wit enough to keep warm."
[20]will ... you: whether you want me or not

Thou must be married to no man but me;
For I am he am born to tame you Kate,
And bring you from a wild Kate[21] to a Kate
Conformable as other household Kates.
Here comes your father. Never make denial.
I must and will have Katharine to my wife.

[21]wild Kate: wild cat

Interpretation

1. Why do you think Katharina is so disagreeable?

2. What type of person is Petruchio? Analyze his character.

3. One of the most important aspects of this cutting is the witty repartee. How would you direct the line delivery?

4. What is the theme of this cutting? The conflict?

5. How do the two characters feel about each other? Pick out specific lines to support this.

6. If you were directing this cutting, how would you like to have the characters react to each other physically?

Act 1

ARMS AND THE MAN

George Bernard Shaw

T his play is an attack on the romantic ideas often associated with war. The central character, Captain Bluntschli, would much rather eat chocolate than fight. In fact, he carries chocolate rather than bullets in his cartridge belt. A comedy, *Arms and the Man* pokes fun at society in general rather than at individuals. Bluntschli is sensible in his deviance from the accepted, showing that the conventional view of war is foolish.

A professional soldier in the Serbian Army, Bluntschli is much more interested in saving his skin than in being a hero.

Raina, the female lead, has a noble bearing but is an unconscionable liar. Her fiancé, Sergius Saranoff, has led a successful charge against the enemy only because they were given the wrong caliber ammunition. He professes love for Raina but makes love to the servants whenever he can.

In this cutting, the Man is Bluntschli, who is attempting to hide in Raina's bedroom. Just before the first line, Raina has sat on the Man's pistol which was on the ottoman. She "jumps up with a shriek. The Man, all nerves, shies like a frightened horse to the other side of the room."

THE MAN [*Irritably.*]: Don't frighten me like that. What is it?

RAINA: Your revolver! It was staring that officer in the face all the time. What an escape!

THE MAN [*Vexed at being unnecessarily terrified.*]: Oh, is that all?

RAINA [*Staring at him rather superciliously as she conceives a poorer and poorer opinion of him, and feels proportionately more and more at her ease.*]: I am sorry I frightened you. [*She takes up the pistol and hands it to him.*] Pray take it to protect yourself against me.

THE MAN [*Grinning wearily at the sarcasm as he takes the pistol.*]:
No use, dear young lady; there's nothing in it. It's not loaded.
[*He makes a grimace at it, and drops it despairingly into his
revolver case.*]

RAINA: Load it by all means.

THE MAN: I've no ammunition. What use are cartridges in battle? I
always carry chocolate instead; and I finished the last cake of
that hours ago.

RAINA [*Outraged in her most cherished ideals of manhood.*]:
Chocolate! Do you stuff your pockets with sweets—like a
schoolboy—even in the field?

THE MAN [*Grinning.*]: Yes: isn't it contemptible? [*Hungrily.*] I wish
I had some now.

RAINA: Allow me. [*She sails away scornfully to the chest of
drawers, and returns with the box of confectionery in her hand.*]
I am sorry I have eaten them all except these. [*She offers him
the box.*]

THE MAN [*Ravenously.*]: You're an angel! [*He gobbles the contents.*]
Creams! Delicious! [*He looks anxiously to see whether there are
any more. There are none: he can only scrape the box with his
fingers and suck them. When that nourishment is exhausted he
accepts the inevitable with pathetic goodhumor, and says, with
grateful emotion:*] Bless you, dear lady! You can always tell an
old soldier by the inside of his holsters and cartridge boxes.
The young ones carry pistols and cartridges: the old ones,
grub. Thank you. [*He hands back the box. She snatches it
contemptuously from him and throws it away. He shies again,
as if she had meant to strike him.*] Ugh! Don't do things so
suddenly, gracious lady. It's mean to revenge yourself because
I frightened you just now.

RAINA [*Loftily.*]: Frighten me! Do you know, sir, that though I am
only a woman, I think I am at heart as brave as you.

THE MAN: I should think so. You haven't been under fire for three
days as I have. I can stand two days without shewing it much;
but no man can stand three days: I'm as nervous as a mouse.
[*He sits down on the ottoman, and takes his head in his
hands.*] Would you like to see me cry?

RAINA [*Alarmed.*]: No.

THE MAN: If you would, all you have to do is to scold me just as if I were a little boy and you my nurse. If I were in camp now, they'd play all sorts of tricks on me.

RAINA [*A little moved.*]: I'm sorry. I won't scold you. [*Touched by the sympathy in her tone, he raises his head and looks gratefully at her: she immediately draws back and says stiffly:*] You must excuse me: our soldiers are not like that. [*She moves away from the ottoman.*]

THE MAN: Oh yes they are. There are only two sorts of soldiers: old ones and young ones. I've served fourteen years: half of your fellows never smelt powder before. Why, how is it that you've just beaten us? Sheer ignorance of the art of war, nothing else. [*Indignantly.*] I never saw anything so unprofessional.

RAINA [*Ironically.*]: Oh! was it unprofessional to beat you?

THE MAN: Well, come! is it professional to throw a regiment of cavalry on a battery of machine guns, with the dead certainty that if the guns go off not a horse or man will ever get within fifty yards of the fire? I couldn't believe my eyes when I saw it.

RAINA [*Eagerly turning to him, as all her enthusiasm and her dreams of glory rush back on her.*]: Did you see the great cavalry charge? Oh, tell me about it. Describe it to me.

THE MAN: You never saw a cavalry charge, did you?

RAINA: How could I?

THE MAN: Ah, perhaps not. No: of course not! Well, it's a funny sight. It's like slinging a handful of peas against a window pane: first one comes; then two or three close behind him; and then all the rest in a lump.

RAINA [*Her eyes dilating as she raises her clasped hands ecstatically.*]: Yes, first One! the bravest of the brave!

THE MAN [*Prosaically.*]: Hm! you should see the poor devil pulling at his horse.

RAINA: Why should he pull at his horse?

THE MAN [*Impatient of so stupid a question.*]: It's running away with him, of course: do you suppose the fellow wants to get there before the others and be killed? Then they all come. You can tell the young ones by their wildness and their slashing. The old ones come bunched up under the number one guard: they know that they're mere projectiles, and that it's no use trying to fight. The wounds are mostly broken knees, from the horses cannoning together.

RAINA: Ugh! But I don't believe the first man is a coward. I know he is a hero!

THE MAN [*Goodhumoredly.*]: That's what you'd have said if you'd seen the first man in the charge today.

RAINA [*Breathless, forgiving him everything.*]: Ah, I knew it! Tell me. Tell me about him.

THE MAN: He did it like an operatic tenor. A regular handsome fellow, with flashing eyes and lovely moustache, shouting his war-cry and charging like Don Quixote at the windmills. We did laugh.

RAINA: You dared to laugh!

THE MAN: Yes; but when the sergeant ran up as white as a sheet, and told us they'd sent us the wrong ammunition, and that we couldn't fire a round for the next ten minutes, we laughed at the other side of our mouths. I never felt so sick in my life; though I've been in one or two very tight places. And I hadn't even a revolver cartridge: only chocolate. We'd no bayonets: nothing. Of course, they just cut us to bits. And there was Don Quixote flourishing like a drum major, thinking he'd done the cleverest thing ever known, whereas he ought to be court-martialled for it. Of all the fools ever let loose on a field of battle, that man must be the very maddest. He and his regiment simply committed suicide; only the pistol missed fire: that's all.

RAINA [*Deeply wounded, but steadfastly loyal to her ideals.*]: Indeed! Would you know him again if you saw him?

THE MAN: Shall I ever forget him!

[*She again goes to the chest of drawers. He watches her with a vague hope that she may have something more for him to eat. She takes the portrait from its stand and brings it to him.*]

RAINA: That is a photograph of the gentleman—the patriot and hero—to whom I am betrothed.

THE MAN [*Recognizing it with a shock.*]: I'm really very sorry. [*Looking at her.*] Was it fair to lead me on? [*He looks at the portrait again.*] Yes: that's Don Quixote: not a doubt of it. [*He stifles a laugh.*]

RAINA [*Quickly.*]: Why do you laugh?

THE MAN [*Apologetic, but still greatly tickled.*]: I didn't laugh, I assure you. At least I didn't mean to. But when I think of him charging the windmills and imagining he was doing the finest thing—[*He chokes with suppressed laughter.*]

RAINA [*Sternly.*]: Give me back the portrait, sir.

THE MAN [*With sincere remorse.*]: Of course. Certainly. I'm really very sorry. [*He hands her the picture. She deliberately kisses it and looks him straight in the face before returning to the chest of drawers to replace it. He follows her, apologizing.*] Perhaps I'm quite wrong, you know: no doubt I am. Most likely he had got wind of the cartridge business somehow, and knew it was a safe job.

RAINA: That is to say, he was a pretender and a coward! You did not dare say that before.

THE MAN [*With a comic gesture of despair.*]: It's no use, dear lady: I can't make you see it from the professional point of view. [*As he turns away to get back to the ottoman, a couple of distant shots threaten renewed trouble.*]

RAINA [*Sternly, as she sees him listening to the shots.*]: So much the better for you!

THE MAN [*Turning.*]: How?

RAINA: You are my enemy; and you are at my mercy. What would I do if I were a professional soldier?

THE MAN: Ah, true, dear young lady: you're always right. I know how good you've been to me: to my last hour I shall remember those three chocolate creams. It was unsoldierly; but it was angelic.

RAINA [*Coldly.*]: Thank you. And now I will do a soldierly thing. You cannot stay here after what you have just said about my future husband; but I will go out on the balcony and see whether it is safe for you to climb down into the street. [*She turns to the window.*]

THE MAN [*Changing countenance.*]: Down that waterpipe! Stop! Wait! I can't! I daren't! The very thought of it makes me giddy. I came up it fast enough with death behind me. But to face it now in cold blood—! [*He sinks on the ottoman.*] It's no use: I give up: I'm beaten. Give the alarm. [*He drops his head on his hands in the deepest dejection.*]

RAINA [*Disarmed by pity.*]: Come: don't be disheartened. [*She stoops over him almost maternally: he shakes his head.*] Oh, you are a very poor soldier: a chocolate cream soldier! Come, cheer up! It takes less courage to climb down than to face capture: remember that.

THE MAN [*Dreamily, lulled by her voice.*]: No: capture only means death; and death is sleep: oh, sleep, sleep, sleep, undisturbed sleep! Climbing down the pipe means doing something— exerting myself—thinking! Death ten times over first.

RAINA [*Softly and wonderingly, catching the rhythm of his weariness.*]: Are you as sleepy as that?

THE MAN: I've not had two hours undisturbed sleep since I joined. I haven't closed my eyes for forty-eight hours.

RAINA [*At her wit's end.*]: But what am I to do with you?

THE MAN [*Staggering up, roused by her desperation.*]: Of course. I must do something. [*He shakes himself; pulls himself together; and speaks with rallied vigor and courage.*] You see, sleep or no sleep, hunger or no hunger, tired or not tired, you can always do a thing when you know it must be done. Well, that pipe must be got down: [*He hits himself on the chest.*] do you hear that, you chocolate cream soldier? [*He turns to the window.*]

RAINA [*Anxiously.*]: But if you fall?

THE MAN: I shall sleep as if the stones were a feather bed. Goodbye. [*He makes boldly for the window; and his hand is on the shutter when there is a terrible burst of firing in the street beneath.*]

RAINA [*Rushing to him.*]: Stop! [*She seizes him recklessly, and pulls him quite round.*] They'll kill you.

THE MAN [*Coolly, but attentively.*]: Never mind: this sort of thing is all in my day's work. I'm bound to take my chance. [*Decisively.*] Now do what I tell you. Put out the candle; so that they shan't see the light when I open the shutters. And keep away from the window, whatever you do. If they see me they're sure to have a shot at me.

RAINA [*Clinging to him.*]: They're sure to see you: it's bright moonlight. I'll save you. Oh, how can you be so indifferent! You want me to save you, don't you?

THE MAN: I really don't want to be troublesome. [*She shakes him in her impatience.*] I am not indifferent, dear young lady, I assure you. But how is it to be done?

RAINA: Come away from the window. [*She takes him firmly back to the middle of the room. The moment she releases him he turns mechanically towards the window again. She seizes him and turns him back, exclaiming:*] Please! [*He becomes motionless, like a hypnotized rabbit, his fatigue gaining fast on him. She releases him, and addresses him patronizingly.*] Now listen. You must trust to our hospitality. You do not yet know in whose house you are. I am a Petkoff.

THE MAN: A pet what?

RAINA [*Rather indignantly.*]: I mean that I belong to the family of the Petkoffs, the richest and best known in our country.

THE MAN: Oh, yes, of course. I beg your pardon. The Petkoffs, to be sure. How stupid of me!

RAINA: You know you never heard of them until this moment. How can you stoop to pretend!

THE MAN: Forgive me: I'm too tired to think; and the change of subject was too much for me. Don't scold me.

RAINA: I forgot. It might make you cry. [*He nods, quite seriously. She pouts and then resumes her patronizing tone.*] I must tell you that my father holds the highest command of any Bulgarian in our army. He is [*Proudly.*] a Major.

THE MAN [*Pretending to be deeply impressed.*]: A Major! Bless me! Think of that!

RAINA: You shewed great ignorance in thinking that it was necessary to climb up to the balcony because ours is the only private house that has two rows of windows. There is a flight of stairs inside to get up and down by.

THE MAN: Stairs! How grand! You live in great luxury indeed, dear young lady.

RAINA: Do you know what a library is?

THE MAN: A library? A roomful of books?

RAINA: Yes. We have one, the only one in Bulgaria.

THE MAN: Actually a real library! I should like to see that.

RAINA [*Affectedly.*]: I tell you these things to shew you that you are not in the house of ignorant country folk who would kill you

Arms and the Man
Photo by Bill Reid
Courtesy of Old Globe Theatre, San Diego, California

the moment they saw your Serbian uniform, but among civilized people. We go to Bucharest every year for the opera season; and I have spent a whole month in Vienna.

THE MAN: I saw that, dear young lady. I saw at once that you knew the world.

RAINA: Have you ever seen the opera of Ernani?

THE MAN: Is that the one with the devil in it in red velvet, and a soldiers' chorus?

RAINA [*Contemptuously.*]: No!

THE MAN [*Stifling a heavy sigh of weariness.*]: Then I don't know it.

RAINA: I thought you might have remembered the great scene where Ernani, flying from his foes just as you are tonight, takes refuge in the castle of his bitterest enemy, an old Castilian noble. The noble refuses to give him up. His guest is sacred to him.

THE MAN [*Quickly, waking up a little.*]: Have your people got that notion?

RAINA [*With dignity.*]: My mother and I can understand that notion, as you call it. And if instead of threatening me with your pistol as you did you had simply thrown yourself as a fugitive on our hospitality, you would have been as safe as in your father's house.

THE MAN: Quite sure?

RAINA [*Turning her back on him in disgust.*]: Oh, it is useless to try to make you understand.

THE MAN: Don't be angry: you see how awkward it would be for me if there was any mistake. My father is a very hospitable man: he keeps six hotels; but I couldn't trust him as far as that. What about your father?

RAINA: He is away at Slivnitza fighting for his country. I answer for your safety. There is my hand in pledge of it. Will that reassure you? [*She offers him her hand.*]

THE MAN [*Looking dubiously at his own hand.*]: Better not touch my hand, dear young lady. I must have a wash first.

RAINA [*Touched.*]: That is very nice of you. I see that you are a gentleman.

THE MAN [*Puzzled.*]: Eh?

RAINA: You must not think I am surprised. Bulgarians of really good standing—people in our position—wash their hands nearly every day. So you see I can appreciate your delicacy. You may take my hand. [*She offers it again.*]

THE MAN [*Kissing it with his hands behind his back.*]: Thanks, gracious young lady: I feel safe at last. And now would you mind breaking the news to your mother? I had better not stay here secretly longer than is necessary.

RAINA: If you will be so good as to keep perfectly still whilst I am away.

THE MAN: Certainly. [*He sits down on the ottoman.*]

[RAINA *goes to the bed and wraps herself in the fur cloak. His eyes close. She goes to the door. Turning for a last look at him, she sees that he is dropping off to sleep.*]

RAINA [*At the door.*]: You are not going asleep, are you?

[*He murmurs inarticulately: she runs to him and shakes him.*] Do you hear? Wake up: you are falling asleep.

THE MAN: Eh? Falling aslee—? Oh no: not the least in the world: I was only thinking. It's all right: I'm wide awake.

RAINA [*Severely.*]: Will you please stand up while I am away. [*He rises reluctantly.*] All the time, mind.

THE MAN [*Standing unsteadily.*]: Certainly. Certainly: you may depend on me.

[RAINA *looks doubtfully at him. He smiles weakly. She goes reluctantly, turning again at the door, and almost catching him in the act of yawning. She goes out.*]

THE MAN [*Drowsily.*]: Sleep, sleep, sleep, sleep, slee—[*The words trail off into a murmur. He wakes again with a shock on the point of falling.*] Where am I? That's what I want to know: where am I? Must keep awake. Nothing keeps me awake except danger: remember that: [*Intently.*] danger, danger, danger, dan—[*Trailing off again: another shock.*] Where's danger? Mus' find it. [*He starts off vaguely round the room in search of it.*] What am I looking for? Sleep—danger—don't know. [*He stumbles against the bed.*] Ah yes: now I know. All right now. I'm to go to bed, but not to sleep. Be sure not to sleep, because of danger. Not to lie down either, only sit down. [*He sits on the bed. A blissful expression comes into his face.*] Ah! [*With a happy sigh he sinks back at full length; lifts his boots into the bed with a final effort; and falls fast asleep instantly.*]

Interpretation

1. What is Raina's most important trait? The Man's?

2. What is the purpose of this cutting? What points does it make? What provides the interest? What important beliefs about war does Shaw express in this cutting? How would you emphasize them for an audience?

3. What is the dominant mood? What feelings would you want to have the audience experience when viewing this cutting?

4. Are the characters believable? Why or why not?

5. Plan out the blocking. Justify your choices.

The Tattoo Parlor

Louis K. Phillips

The cutting is from the opening of the play, most of which is performed by only two characters. Later, a third character, Warren Hampden, enters. He is Darlene's fiancé. She has come to the tattoo parlor because she feels he does not really appreciate her, and so she wants to do something that will shock him.

[*There is the sound of a car pulling up, a door closing. A woman appears in the doorway. An apparition. Almost. She is* DARLENE META, *20 to 21 years old, dressed in a very proper skirt-and-blouse combination; she is definitely out of her element.*]

DARLENE: Is this really a tattoo parlor?

[CARLETON *is too stunned to reply.*]

DARLENE: Yoo-hoo.

CARLETON: You talking to me, lady?

DARLENE: Is this where people come to get tattooed?

CARLETON: I guess so. I know they don't come here to buy groceries.

DARLENE: Good. Stay where you are and I'll be right back. . . . I just have to pay the cab-driver. . . . Don't go away.

CARLETON: Wait a minute, lady!

[*Too late. The apparition has vanished.*]

CARLETON: I'm not open for business now. I just had the door open so I could listen to the rain.

[DARLENE *returns carrying a small green suitcase and an umbrella. We hear the cab driving off.*]

CARLETON: I wouldn't let that cab go if I were you.

DARLENE: Why not?

CARLETON: Because . . . Oh forget it.

[*In the light we can see that* DARLENE *has been crying, her eyes are slightly puffed.*]

DARLENE: Can I put my suitcase down?

CARLETON: As long as you're not planning to move in.

DARLENE: You don't know how glad I am to find a place like this. I've been looking all over for a tattoo parlor, and the cab-driver remembered that there was one down by the docks.

CARLETON: You're not a lawyer by any chance?

DARLENE: I'm going to be an architect.

CARLETON: Oh.

DARLENE: Why?

CARLETON: Because as soon as somebody says that they've been looking all over for me, I know it means trouble.

[CARLETON *closes the door.*]

DARLENE: Why did you close the door?

CARLETON: There are not too many things to do with a door. You open it. You close it. I usually close it when I have a client. What's the matter? You frightened?

DARLENE [*Frightened.*]: No. I'm not frightened. Your place just seems different with the door closed.

CARLETON: You should have seen it before the roof was put on. Look, if it'll make you feel any better, I'll keep the door open. [*He opens the door.*] But if anybody sees somebody like you in here, they'll just come walking right in, and some of them are pretty rough. All I guarantee is the permanence of the tattoo. I can't guarantee the personal safety of my customers. I used to have a sign that said it, but it's been torn down.

DARLENE: You're right. Perhaps you'd better keep it closed.

CARLETON [*Closing the door.*]: I don't care which. Just make up your mind. After all, I didn't invite you here.

DARLENE: You didn't seem to be afraid of people walking in on you.

CARLETON: If I were in a different line of business, I'd be afraid, but, as it is, nobody steals tattoos. . . . Want a beer?

DARLENE: No, thank you. It took me three drinks to get here. . . . Pink Ladies.

CARLETON: How about some tea. I'll put some tea on.

DARLENE: Tea?

CARLETON: Yeah, you know. Tea . . . Help dry you out.

DARLENE: Oh no. You're not going to drug me and sell me to some white slave trader. Just give me my tattoos and I'll go home.

CARLETON: Just give you your tattoos and you'll go home. What do you think I do, lady? Just put it in a paper-sack like a chicken-salad sandwich? Tattooing isn't done like that.

DARLENE: Why must everything be so complicated? When my brother and I were growing up, we'd buy these pictures for a penny, spit on them, and rub them right on to our skin.

CARLETON: If you want something like that, you go to a dime store, not a tattoo parlor.

DARLENE: You call this a parlor?

CARLETON: I wasn't planning on entertaining Queen Victoria tonight.

DARLENE: There's no need to take that tone with me.

CARLETON: Well, we don't spit on our tattoos around here.

[He finds a glass, spits into it to clean it for the tea, wipes it out with his shirt.]

DARLENE: I think I'll pass up the tea.

CARLETON: Pass up the tattooing while you're at it.

DARLENE: Oh no. You're not going to talk me out of it. I know what I want. I want to be made exotic. No man is ever going to call me dull and uninteresting again. I'll show him.

CARLETON: Is that why you've been crying? Because some man said you were uninteresting?

DARLENE: Do you think I've been crying?

CARLETON: You look like you've been crying.

DARLENE: Are my eyes all puffy? I hate it when my eyes get all puffy.

CARLETON: What's your name?

DARLENE: There's no need to get intimate. I just want a tattoo.

CARLETON: I just asked.

DARLENE: If I wanted counselling, I could have gone to the YWCA.

CARLETON: You certainly would have been better off there than running around deserted docks at two o'clock in the morning.

DARLENE: My name is Darlene and it's not two o'clock in the morning.

[CARLETON *pulls out a silver pocket watch and snaps it open.*]

CARLETON: Not in Hawaii, it's not. But here it's 1:47 . . . But then Boston has always been a bit behind the rest of the world.

DARLENE: I didn't realize it was that late.

CARLETON: If you missed it the first time, it'll come around again.

Interpretation

1. What provides the tension in this cutting? The conflict?

2. What is Darlene's state of mind? How would you make sure the audience grasps this?

3. Is Carleton a likeable person? Why do you think so?

4. Who is the dominant character in this cutting? Why do you think so? How would you establish this for an audience?

5. From what is given, analyze Carleton's and Darlene's characters.

Act 3, scene 1

Fashion

Anna Cora Mowatt Ritchie

O ne of the first American plays dealing with social satire, *Fash-ion,* which opened in New York in 1845, set the precedent for a series of similar plays that followed. The author took aim at a num-ber of "types" still satirized today. The major type, apparent in the following scene, is, of course, the social climber.

The play deals with Mrs. Tiffany's affectations of high society after her husband's success as a merchant.

[MRS. TIFFANY's *Parlor. Enter* MRS. TIFFANY, *followed by* MR. TIFFANY.]

TIFFANY: Your extravagance will ruin me, Mrs. Tiffany!

MRS. TIFFANY: And your stinginess will ruin me, Mr. Tiffany! It is totally and *toot a fate*[1] impossible to convince you of the necessity of *keeping up appearances*. There is a certain display which every woman of fashion is forced to make!

TIFFANY: And pray who made *you* a woman of fashion?

MRS. TIFFANY: What a vulgar question! All women of fashion, Mr. Tiffany—

TIFFANY: In this land are *self-constituted,* like you, Madam—and *fashion* is the cloak for more sins than charity ever covered! It was for *fashion's* sake that you insisted upon my purchasing this expensive house—it was for *fashion's* sake that you ran me in debt at every exorbitant upholsterer's and extravagant furniture warehouse in the city—it was for *fashion's* sake that you built that ruinous conservatory—hired more servants than they have persons to wait upon—and dressed your footman like a harlequin!

[1]toot a fate: tout à fait (French); quite. The spelling indicates a mispronun-ciation.

MRS. TIFFANY: Mr. Tiffany, you are thoroughly plebeian, and insufferably *American,* in your grovelling ideas! And, pray, what was the occasion for these very *mal-ap-pro-pos* remarks? Merely because I requested a paltry fifty dollars to purchase a new style of head-dress—a *bijou*[2] of an article just introduced in France.

TIFFANY: Time was, Mrs. Tiffany, when you manufactured your own French head-dresses—took off their first gloss at the public balls, and then sold them to your shortest-sighted customers. And all you knew about France, or French either, was what you spelt out at the bottom of your fashion plates— but now you have grown so fashionable, forsooth, that you have forgotten how to speak your mother tongue!

MRS. TIFFANY: Mr. Tiffany, Mr. Tiffany! Nothing is more positively vulgarian—more *unaristocratic* than any allusion to the past!

TIFFANY: Why I thought, my dear, that *aristocrats* lived principally upon the past—and traded in the market of fashion with the bones of their ancestors for capital?

MRS. TIFFANY: Mr. Tiffany, such vulgar remarks are only suitable to the counting house, in my drawing room you should—

TIFFANY: Vary my sentiments with my locality, as you change your *manners* with your *dress!*

MRS. TIFFANY: Mr. Tiffany, I desire that you will purchase Count d'Orsay's "Science of Etiquette," and learn how to conduct yourself—especially before you appear at the grand ball, which I shall give on Friday!

TIFFANY: Confound your balls, Madam; they make *footballs* of my money, while you dance away all that I am worth! A pretty time to give a ball when you know that I am on the very brink of bankruptcy!

MRS. TIFFANY: So much the greater reason that nobody should suspect your circumstances, or you would lose your credit at once. Just at this crisis a ball is absolutely *necessary* to save your reputation! There is Mrs. Adolphus Dashaway—she gave the most splendid fête of the season—and I hear on very good authority that her husband has not paid his baker's bill in three months. Then there was Mrs. Honeywood—

TIFFANY: Gave a ball the night before her husband shot himself— perhaps you wish to drive me to follow his example? [*Crosses.*]

[2]bijou: delicate or elegant

MRS. TIFFANY: Good gracious! Mr. Tiffany, how you talk! I beg you won't mention anything of the kind. I consider black the most unbecoming color. I'm sure I've done all that I could to gratify you. There is that vulgar old torment, Trueman, who gives one the lie fifty times a day—haven't I been very civil to him?

TIFFANY: Civil to his *wealth,* Mrs. Tiffany! I told you that he was a rich, old farmer—the early friend of my father—my own benefactor—and that I had reason to think he might assist me in my present embarrassments. Your civility was *bought*—and like most of your *own* purchases has yet to be *paid* for. [*Crosses.*]

MRS. TIFFANY: And will be, no doubt! The condescension of a woman of fashion should command any price. Mr. Trueman is insupportably indecorous—he has insulted Count Jolimaitre in the most outrageous manner. If the Count was not so deeply interested—so *abîmé*³ with Seraphina, I am sure he would never honor us by his visits again!

TIFFANY: So much the better—he shall never marry my daughter!—I am resolved on that. Why, Madam, I am told there is in Paris a regular matrimonial stock company, who fit out indigent dandies for this market. How do I know but this fellow is one of its creatures, and that he has come here to increase its dividends by marrying a fortune?

MRS. TIFFANY: Nonsense, Mr. Tiffany. The Count, the most fashionable young man in all New York—the intimate friend of all the dukes and lords in Europe—not marry my daughter? Not permit Seraphina to become a Countess? Mr. Tiffany, you are out of your senses!

TIFFANY: That would not be very wonderful, considering how many years I have been united to you, my dear. Modern physicians pronounce lunacy infectious!

³abîmé: (French) spoiled, damaged. Mrs. Tiffany is misusing the word.

Interpretation

1. What elements of this scene show beyond any doubt that the play is a comedy? How would you emphasize these elements?

2. As mentioned in the introduction to the play, the author deals with types. Yet, the characters also must be presented as individuals. How would you point up the typical aspects of these two characters, while at the same time individualizing them?

3. Who is the stronger of the two characters in this scene? What makes you think so?

4. What provides the conflict in the scene? How would you point it up? What are the emotions of each character? How would you portray this for an audience?

5. How would you position the actors in this scene? Why?

Act 2, scene 6

Cyrano de Bergerac

Edmond Rostand

C yrano is in love with his cousin Roxane. But he cannot tell her
so, he feels, because of his physical deformity, a grotesque nose.
When she begins to love Christian, Cyrano helps the young man win
her. After Christian dies in battle, Cyrano resolves not to let Roxane
discover that he was the real soul behind Christian's wooing.

Cyrano remains devoted to Roxane after she becomes a nun. Then,
wounded by enemies, and near death, he finally comes to her and
confesses what he's done.

Translated by Howard Thayer Kingsbury

CYRANO: Now let this moment be most blest of all,
When, ceasing to forget I humbly breathe,
You come to say to me—to say to me—

ROXANE [*After having unmasked.*]: To thank you first,
because the knavish dolt
Whom you put to the laugh, with your good sword,
Is he whom a great lord—in love with me—

CYRANO: De Guiche!

ROXANE [*Lowering her eyes.*]: has tried to give me—for a husband.

CYRANO: So-called?
[*Bowing.*] Then I have fought, and better so,
For your bright eyes, not for my ugly nose.

ROXANE: And then—I wished—but to make this avowal
I needs must see in you the—almost brother,
With whom I played, in the park, by the lake!

CYRANO: Yes; you came every year to Bergerac.

ROXANE: The reeds then furnished you with wood for swords.

CYRANO: And the corn, yellow hair to deck your dolls.

ROXANE: Those were the days of games—

CYRANO: —of berry-picking—

ROXANE: The days when you did all things that I wished!

CYRANO: Roxane, in dresses short, was called Madeleine.

ROXANE: And I was pretty then?

CYRANO: You were not ugly.

ROXANE: Sometimes, when you had cut your hand in climbing
You ran to me; then I would play the mother,
And say with voice that tried hard to be stern
[*Takes his hand.*]
"What is this scratch now?"
[*Stops in amazement.*] Ah, too bad! And this?
[CYRANO *tries to draw back his hand.*]
No! Show it to me! What? At your age, still?
How came it?

CYRANO: Playing, at the Porte de Nesle.

ROXANE [*Sitting at a table and dipping her handkerchief in a glass of water.*]: Come!

CYRANO [*Also sitting down.*]: Like a fond and happy little mother!

ROXANE: And tell me, while I wipe away the blood,
How many were there?

CYRANO: Oh! Not quite a hundred.

ROXANE: Tell me!

CYRANO: No, let it go! But you tell me
That which just now you dared not—

ROXANE [*Without letting go of his hand.*]: Now I dare.
The past's sweet odor gives me courage new.
Yes, now I dare. Listen, I love someone.

CYRANO: Ah!

ROXANE: Who has not guessed it!

CYRANO: Ah!

ROXANE: At least, not yet.

CYRANO: Ah!

ROXANE: But who soon will know, if he knows it not.

CYRANO: Ah!

ROXANE: A poor lad, who has loved me until now
Timidly, from afar, nor dared to speak.

CYRANO: Ah!

ROXANE: Leave me your hand, it is all feverish!—
But I have seen love trembling on his lips.

CYRANO: Ah!

ROXANE [*Finishing a little bandage for him made of her
handkerchief.*]: And do you know, my cousin, that in fact
He now is serving in your regiment!

CYRANO: Ah!

ROXANE [*Smiling.*]: In your own company he's a cadet!

CYRANO: Ah!

ROXANE: His forehead shows his genius and his wit,
He's young, proud, noble, brave, and fair—

CYRANO [*Getting up, very pale.*]: What, fair?

ROXANE: Why, what's the matter?

CYRANO: Nothing—'tis—[*With a smile, showing his hand.*]—this
wound.

ROXANE: In fine, I love him. I must tell you, too,
That I have seen him only at the play—

CYRANO: You have not spoken?

ROXANE: Only with our eyes.

CYRANO: How do you know him then?

ROXANE: Under the lindens,
In the Place Royale, there is talk; and gossip
Has told me—

CYRANO: He is a cadet?

ROXANE: He is.
He's in the Guards.

CYRANO: His name?

ROXANE: The Baron Christian
De Neuvillette—

CYRANO: What? He's not in the Guards.

Cyrano de Bergerac
Photo courtesy of Kent State University Theatre, Kent, Ohio

ROXANE: Yes, since this morning, under Captain Carbon
De Castel-Jaloux.

CYRANO: Ah! how quick is love!
But my poor child—

THE DUENNA [*Opening the door in the background.*]:
Monsieur de Bergerac,
I've finished all the cakes.

CYRANO: Well, read the verses
Upon the bags. [*The* DUENNA *disappears.*]
My poor child, you who love
Keen wit and courtly speech, if he should be
A man unlearned, unpolished, in the rough!

ROXANE: No, he has hair like one of D'Urfé's heroes!

CYRANO: His speech may lack the grace his hair displays!

ROXANE: No, every word he speaks I know is brilliant.

CYRANO: Yes, words are brilliant from a fair moustache;
But if he were a dolt!—

ROXANE [*Tapping with her foot.*]: Then I should die!

CYRANO [*After a pause.*]: So you have brought me here to tell me that.
I cannot see the good of it, Madame!

ROXANE: Ah! yesterday I had a deadly shock,—
I heard that you are Gascons, every one,
All of your company—

CYRANO: And that we pick
Quarrels with all recruits, who by mere favor
Gain entrance to our ranks of Gascon blood,
And are not Gascons? That is what you heard?

ROXANE: Think how I trembled for him!

CYRANO [*Between his teeth.*]: With good reason!

ROXANE: But yesterday when you appeared to us
So mighty and so brave, holding your own
Against the rabble, punishing that knave,
I thought—if he but would, whom all men fear—

CYRANO: 'Tis well, I will protect your little baron.

ROXANE: Ah, then you will protect him well for me?
I've always had so warm a friendship for you!

CYRANO: Yes, yes.

ROXANE: You'll be his friend?

CYRANO: I'll be his friend.

ROXANE: And he shall fight no duels?

CYRANO: On my oath!

ROXANE: I am so fond of you! Now I must go. [*Quickly puts on her mask, and a bit of lace over her head, and absent-mindedly:*] But you have not yet told me of the battle Last night. It must have been a mighty feat— Tell him to write. [*Throws him a little kiss with her fingers.*] I am so fond of you.

CYRANO: Yes, yes.

ROXANE: Five score against you? Well, good-by, We are great friends?

CYRANO: Yes, yes.

ROXANE: Tell him to write. A hundred! You will tell me later. Now I cannot stay. A hundred! Oh! what courage!

CYRANO [*Bowing to her.*]: I have done better since.

Interpretation

1. What can you tell about Roxane's character that is not stated in words? How can you convey this to an audience?

2. Knowing Cyrano really is in love with Roxane, how would you have him play this scene? What emotions would he feel? What would you want the audience to feel?

3. Do you think the theme provides a good basis for a play? Why or why not?

4. What provides the tension in this cutting? The conflict?

5. What type of setting would you use for this cutting to convey the mood and atmosphere? What type of costumes?

Cuttings for Three Persons

The Beggar's Opera

The Imaginary Invalid

Death of a Salesman

Riders to the Sea

Blood Wedding

The Imaginary Invalid
Photo by David Weeks
Courtesy of Grossmont College Drama Department,
El Cajon, California

Act 1, scene 8

The Beqqar's Opera

John Gay

The play is both a burlesque of Italian opera and a satire on the politics of the time, the late 1720s. A great deal of the humor depends on the fact that all of the characters, in one way or another, are on the wrong side of the law. Still, they live by a certain standard of ethics.

The premise is comparable to the contemporary *White Sheep of the Family,* in which all the family members are thieves. Yet they are conscientious about their work because they believe that hard work is the key to success.

Gay seems to be suggesting that criminals are no more wrong in the way they approach life than are any hard-working people. Of course, rather than containing any great social message, the play exists mainly for entertainment.

One of the criminals is Macheath, handsome, romantic, and courageous. He woos and marries Polly Peachum, daughter of a politician who serves both police and outlaw. Macheath is one of his clients, so Peachum and his wife have no objection to the romance between Polly and Macheath. But the marriage, done in secret, is another thing.

MRS. PEACHUM [*In a very great Passion.*]: You Baggage! you Hussy! you inconsiderate Jade! had you been hang'd, it would not have vex'd me, for that might have been your Misfortune; but to do such a mad thing by Choice! The Wench is married, Husband.

PEACHUM: Married! The Captain is a bold man, and will risque any thing for Money; to be sure he believes her a Fortune. Do you think your Mother and I should have liv'd comfortably so long together, if ever we had been married? Baggage!

MRS. PEACHUM: I knew she was always a proud Slut; and now the Wench hath play'd the Fool and married, because forsooth she would do like the Gentry. Can you support the expence of a Husband, Hussy, in gaming, drinking and whoring? have you Money enough to carry on the daily Quarrels of Man and Wife about who shall squander most? There are not many Husbands and Wifes, who can bear the Charges of plaguing one another in a handsome way. If you must be married, could you introduce no-body into our Family but a Highwayman? Why, thou foolish Jade, thou wilt be as ill-us'd, and as much neglected, as if thou hadst married a Lord!

PEACHUM: Let not your Anger, my dear, break through the Rules of Decency, for the Captain looks upon himself in the Military Capacity, as a Gentleman by his Profession. Besides what he hath already, I know he is in a fair way of getting, or of dying; and both these ways, let me tell you, are most excellent Chances for a Wife. Tell me, Hussy, are you ruin'd or no?

MRS. PEACHUM: With Polly's Fortune, she might very well have gone off to a Person of Distinction. Yes, that you might, you pouting Slut!

PEACHUM: What, is the Wench dumb? Speak, or I'll make you plead by squeezing out an answer from you. Are you really bound Wife to him, or are you only upon liking? [*Pinches her.*]

POLLY: Oh! [*Screaming.*]

MRS. PEACHUM: How the Mother is to be pitied who hath handsome Daughters! Locks, Bolts, Bars, and Lectures of Morality are nothing to them: They break through them all. They have as much Pleasure in cheating a Father and Mother, as in cheating at Cards.

PEACHUM: Why, Polly, I shall soon know if you are married, by Macheath's keeping from our House.

AIR

POLLY: *Can Love be controul'd by Advice?*
Will Cupid our Mothers obey?
Though my Heart were as frozen as Ice,
At his Flame 'twould have melted away.
When he kist me so closely he prest,
'Twas so sweet that I must have comply'd:
So I thought it both safest and best
To marry, for fear you should chide.

MRS. PEACHUM: Then all the Hopes of our Family are gone for ever and ever!

PEACHUM: And Macheath may hang his Father and Mother-in-Law, in hope to get into their Daughter's Fortune.

POLLY: I did not marry him (as 'tis the Fashion) cooly and deliberately for Honour or Money. But, I love him.

MRS. PEACHUM: Love him! worse and worse! I thought the Girl had been better bred. Oh Husband, Husband! her Folly makes me mad! my Head swims! I'm distracted! I can't support myself— Oh! [*Faints*.]

PEACHUM: See, Wench, to what a Condition you have reduc'd your poor Mother! a Glass of Cordial, this instant. How the poor Woman takes it to Heart!
[POLLY *goes out, and returns with it*.]
Ah, Hussy, now this is the only Comfort your Mother has left!

POLLY: Give her another Glass, Sir; my Mama drinks double the Quantity whenever she is out of Order. This, you see, fetches her.

MRS. PEACHUM: The Girl shows such a Readiness, and so much Concern, that I could almost find in my heart to forgive her.

AIR

O Polly, you might have toy'd and kist.
By keeping Men off, you keep them on.
POLLY: But he so teaz'd me,
And he so pleas'd me,
What I did, you must have done.

MRS. PEACHUM: Not with a Highwayman.—You sorry Slut!

PEACHUM: A Word with you, Wife. 'Tis no new thing for a Wench to take a Man without consent of Parents. You know 'tis the Frailty of Woman, my Dear.

MRS. PEACHUM: Yes, indeed, the Sex is frail. But the first time a Woman is frail, she should be somewhat nice methinks, for then or never is the time to make her Fortune. After that, she hath nothing to do but to guard herself from being found out, and she may do what she pleases.

PEACHUM: Make your self a little easy; I have a Thought shall soon set all Matters again to rights. Why so melancholy, Polly, since what is done cannot be undone, we must all endeavour to make the best of it.

MRS. PEACHUM: Well, Polly; as far as one Woman can forgive another, I forgive thee.—Your Father is too fond of you, Hussy.

POLLY: Then all my Sorrows are at an end.

MRS. PEACHUM: A mighty likely Speech in troth, for a Wench who is just married!

AIR

POLLY: *I, like a Ship in Storms, was tost;*
Yet afraid to put in to Land;
For seiz'd in the Port the Vessel's lost,
Whose Treasure is contreband.
The Waves are laid,
My Duty's paid.
O Joy beyond Expression!
this, safe a-shore,
I ask no more,
My All is in my Possession.

PEACHUM: I hear Customers in t'other Room; Go, talk with 'em, Polly; but come to us again, as soon as they are gone.—But, heark ye, Child, if 'tis the Gentleman who was here Yesterday about the Repeating-Watch; say, you believe we can't get Intelligence of it, till to-morrow. For I lent it to Suky Straddle, to make a Figure with it to-night at a Tavern in Drury-Lane. If t'other Gentleman calls for the Silverhilted Sword; you know Beetle-brow'd Jemmy hath it on, and he doth not come from Tunbridge till Tuesday Night; so that it cannot be had till then.

Interpretation

1. What are the important traits of Mrs. Peachum, Peachum, and Polly that you would want to convey to an audience? What aspects of the cutting do you think could be exaggerated for comic effect? How would you present these aspects?

2. What is the theme of the cutting? What feelings would you want an audience to experience while viewing it?

3. What type of setting and costumes would you use for this cutting? Why?

4. What provides the major conflict? Secondary conflict? Explain.

Act 1

THE IMAGINARY INVALID

Molière

Molière often was called the French Shakespeare, although, unlike his English counterpart, he wrote only comedies. His plays are still frequently produced.

This play, his last, centers around Argan, a wealthy man, who affects severe illness in order to gain attention. Because he is so self-indulgent and obsessive about his would-be ailments, he is a perfect target for medical charlatans. His second wife does not love him but hopes to inherit his fortune when he is killed by the doctor's supposed cures.

Argan hopes to see his daughter, Angelica, married to a man in the medical profession, not realizing she loves someone else. She does, however, care deeply for her father.

It has been said that Molière wrote the play partly as a means of poking fun at himself for his own illness, even though it was quite real. Associated with an acting troupe for whom he wrote, Molière often played his own characters. While playing Argan he was seized with a fit or attack, finished the play, but died shortly after the final curtain. Some believe he may have had tuberculosis.

The third character in this cutting is Toinette, a saucy servant who is on to the fact that Argan is really a hypochondriac.

Translated by Miles Malleson

ANGELICA: Darling Father!

TOINETTE: Oh my dear Master!

ARGAN [*Quite taken by surprise.*]: Eh!? What's all this about??

TOINETTE: How are you feeling now?

ARGAN: Weak. Very weak—What's left of me!

TOINETTE: Come and sit down.

ANGELICA: Let me help you.

TOINETTE: Lean on me.

ANGELICA: And me!

[*In their eagerness to get him back into his chair, they almost drag him across the room.*]

ARGAN: Hi! Not so fast! What's all this hurry!

[*So the girls slow up a little.*]

TOINETTE [*With great concern.*]: That's right. Gently does it!

ANGELICA: Careful!!

[*And so they reach his great chair.*]

TOINETTE [*Lowering him into it.*]: Hold on to me.

ANGELICA: And me.

[*He gets into the chair. . . . The girls continue to fuss over him.*]

TOINETTE: *No!* . . . Well! . . . Who'd have thought it. Oh no. I don't believe it, you're making it up.

ARGAN [*Livid; shouting at her.*]: I'm *not* making it up.

ANGELICA: Asked in marriage! [*And out of sheer relief and joy, she breaks into a laugh.*]

ARGAN: You laugh! You like the idea. Find it amusing! Oh Well, you're growing up—it's only natural. So you're pleased.

ANGELICA: Father, even if I wasn't, I'm your daughter, I should obey you.

ARGAN: I should hope so! I'd see to that! Still, I'm glad you're pleased. It makes it easier for me.

TOINETTE: For *you?*

ARGAN [*To Angelica.*]: Your step-mother was against it; wanted to make a Nun of you.

ANGELICA: A Nun?

ARGAN: —send you to a Convent. You, and your little sister!

ANGELICA: But why?

TOINETTE [*Knowingly.*]: No doubt she had her reasons.

ARGAN: But I put my foot down. And to stop all argument, and such unpleasantness, I've arranged to have you married as soon as possible.

TOINETTE: O dear Monsieur Argan, this is the best, the wisest thing you've ever done! Oh, I'm so proud of you! Now, what can I do for you—what about a little drop of medicine!

ARGAN: Medicine! Why?

TOINETTE: To celebrate.

ARGAN: Which?

TOINETTE: The nastiest!

ARGAN: Eh?

TOINETTE: You always say that does you the most good.

ANGELICA: No. Give him the nicest—and a double dose! Oh, father—I'm so grateful.

ARGAN: So you ought to be! Well, that's all settled. I haven't seen the lad, but from what I'm told, when you set eyes on him, you'll be well satisfied.

ANGELICA [*Thoughtlessly.*]: Oh, yes, I shall! I shall!

[*At which Toinette begins to make violent signs of caution to her, behind Argan's back.*]

ARGAN: You seem very certain! How can you be so sure? [*Then he catches the signs, and looks from one to the other of the girls.*] What's all this? What's going on? . . . And now, young lady, perhaps you'll tell me why you're so sure you'll be "well-satisfied."

ANGELICA [*Haltingly.*]: . . . Well . . . you see, father it's like this. . . . Recently—and quite by chance—we met.

ARGAN: You've met??

TOINETTE: In company.

ARGAN: Hold your tongue! . . . What happened?

ANGELICA: Nothing!

ARGAN: Nothing?

ANGELICA: We looked at one another.

ARGAN: Didn't you speak? Did neither say a word?

ANGELICA: Only a very few.

ARGAN: What kind of words?

ANGELICA: A greeting, and goodbye.

ARGAN: I see no harm in that. I'm glad you liked the look of him. They say he's handsome.

ANGELICA [*Ecstatic again.*]: I've never seen a man who's half so handsome!

ARGAN: And clever with it.

ANGELICA: I've never known a man who's half so clever!

ARGAN: He seems to have made an impression! But for once you're right. He must be clever to talk Latin and Greek.

ANGELICA: Latin and Greek!!

ARGAN: Yes.

ANGELICA: He never told me that.

ARGAN: You surprise me! You meet—in company; look at one another; say a few words—and he never told you he spoke Latin and Greek! Still, you might have guessed.

ANGELICA: Guessed?

ARGAN: If he's to take his Doctor's Degree in a few days—he *must* know Latin and Greek.

ANGELICA: Doctor's Degree?

ARGAN: Yes.

ANGELICA: In a few days?

ARGAN: Yes.

ANGELICA: Father—are you sure?

ARGAN: Of course I am!

ANGELICA: But how do you know? Who told you?

ARGAN: My doctor. Doctor Purgon.

ANGELICA: Doctor Purgon! Does Doctor Purgon know him?

ARGAN: Don't be so silly! What a ridiculous question. "Does Doctor Purgon know him!" Not know his own nephew!

ANGELICA: Nephew! Cléante—Doctor Purgon's nephew.

ARGAN: *Cléante?* Who's Cléante, if you please. Cléante, Cléante, Cléante!! Never heard of him. I'm talking of the man you're going to marry.

ANGELICA: And so am I.

TOINETTE: I knew it! You're not talking of the same young man.

ARGAN: Oh, yes I am!

TOINETTE: But *who?!* Who are you talking of?

ARGAN: Why—young Thomas Diaforus. Son of the great Doctor Diaforus.

ANGELICA: Oh, *no!!!!*

TOINETTE: That young Booby!

ARGAN: BOOBY??

TOINETTE: *BOOBY!!!*

ARGAN [*Yelling at her again.*]: Will you be quiet!

TOINETTE: And let you play havoc with your daughter's life! Not me.

ARGAN: Not you, indeed! And what's it got to do with you? Answer me that! No. Don't. I'll not argue with you. I'll not demean myself. I'll not say a word to you. Not a single word.

Interpretation

1. What provides the tension in this cutting? The conflict?

2. Are the three characters realistic? Why or why not?

3. Describe the dominant traits of Argan, Toinette, and Angelica. Analyze their characters.

4. How would you block this scene? What type of set would you prefer?

5. What type of pacing do you think would be most effective? Why? What type of movement?

6. What is the dominant mood of the cutting? What would you want an audience to feel while viewing it?

Act 1

DEATH OF A SALESMAN

Arthur Miller

I n this play Willy Loman, the title character, wants more than
anything to be a success, which he defines in terms of having
money and being well-liked. He deludes himself into thinking that
he is a great salesman.

The three characters in this cutting are Willy's wife, Linda, and
his two sons, Happy and Biff. Although Linda never disagrees with
Willy and constantly makes excuses for his erratic behavior, she
does recognize that he has tried to kill himself. His motive is to
provide insurance money, his definition of success, for his family.

LINDA: He's dying, Biff.

[HAPPY *turns quickly to her, shocked.*]

BIFF [*After a pause.*]: Why is he dying?

LINDA: He's been trying to kill himself.

BIFF [*With great horror.*]: How?

LINDA: I live from day to day.

BIFF: What're you talking about?

LINDA: Remember I wrote you that he smashed up the car again?
In February?

BIFF: Well?

LINDA: The insurance inspector came. He said that they have
evidence. That all these accidents in the last year—weren't—
weren't—accidents.

HAPPY: How can they tell that? That's a lie.

LINDA: It seems there's a woman . . . [*She takes a breath as*

BIFF [*Sharply but contained.*]: What woman?

LINDA [*Simultaneously.*]: . . . and this woman . . .

LINDA: What?

BIFF: Nothing. Go ahead.

LINDA: What did you say?

BIFF: Nothing. I just said what woman?

HAPPY: What about her?

LINDA: Well, it seems she was walking down the road and saw his car. She says that he wasn't driving fast at all, and that he didn't skid. She says he came to that little bridge, and then deliberately smashed into the railing, and it was only the shallowness of the water that saved him.

BIFF: Oh, no, he probably just fell asleep again.

LINDA: I don't think he fell asleep.

BIFF: Why not?

LINDA: Last month . . . [*With great difficulty.*] Oh, boys, it's so hard to say a thing like this! He's just a big stupid man to you, but I tell you there's more good in him than in many other people. [*She chokes, wipes her eyes.*] I was looking for a fuse. The lights blew out, and I went down the cellar. And behind the fuse box—it happened to fall out—was a length of rubber pipe—just short.

HAPPY: No kidding?

LINDA: There's a little attachment on the end of it. I knew right away. And sure enough, on the bottom of the water heater there's a new little nipple on the gas pipe.

HAPPY [*Angrily.*]: That—jerk.

BIFF: Did you have it taken off?

LINDA: I'm—I'm ashamed to. How can I mention it to him? Every day I go down and take away that little rubber pipe. But, when he comes home, I put it back where it was. How can I insult him that way? I don't know what to do. I live from day to day, boys. I tell you, I know every thought in his mind. It sounds so old-fashioned and silly, but I tell you he put his whole life into you and you've turned your backs on him. [*She is bent over in the chair, weeping, her face in her hands.*] Biff, I swear to God! Biff, his life is in your hands!

HAPPY [*To* BIFF.]: How do you like that damned fool!

BIFF [*Kissing her.*]: All right, pal, all right. It's all settled now. I've been remiss. I know that, Mom. But now I'll stay, and I swear to you, I'll apply myself. [*Kneeling in front of her, in a fever of self-reproach.*] It's just—you see, Mom, I don't fit in business. Not that I won't try. I'll try, and I'll make good.

HAPPY: Sure you will. The trouble with you in business was you never tried to please people.

BIFF: I know, I—

HAPPY: Like when you worked for Harrison's. Bob Harrison said you were tops, and then you go and do some damn fool thing like whistling whole songs in the elevator like a comedian.

BIFF [*Against* HAPPY.]: So what? I like to whistle sometimes.

HAPPY: You don't raise a guy to a responsible job who whistles in the elevator!

LINDA: Well, don't argue about it now.

HAPPY: Like when you'd go off and swim in the middle of the day instead of taking the line around.

BIFF [*His resentment rising.*]: Well, don't you run off? You take off sometimes, don't you? On a nice summer day?

HAPPY: Yeah, but I cover myself!

LINDA: Boys!

HAPPY: If I'm going to take a fade the boss can call any number where I'm supposed to be and they'll swear to him that I just left. I'll tell you something that I hate to say, Biff, but in the business world some of them think you're crazy.

Interpretation

1. What sort of an atmosphere would you want to create for the audience with this cutting?

2. What are the goals of each of the characters?

3. What is the theme or central idea in this cutting?

4. Why do you think Biff and Happy get off the subject of Willy's attempted suicide and talk about their own lives? Is this logical? Why or why not?

5. Do you like Linda? Biff? Happy? Why or why not?

6. What emotions are each of the characters feeling in this cutting?

7. What provides the tension in this cutting? How would you convey this to an audience?

Riders to the Sea

John Millington Synge

A highly condensed play, *Riders to the Sea* paints a vivid portrait of the common people of Ireland, for whom the playwright obviously had great feeling. Only what is necessary to the unfolding of the tragedy is included. The dialogue, though poetic, helps paint the picture of the women. By showing the mother's grief over the loss of her husband and sons, Synge powerfully dramatizes the universal experience of grief. The play has often been called the most nearly perfect one-act ever written.

CATHLEEN [*After spinning for a moment.*]: You didn't give him his bit of bread? [MAURYA *begins to keen softly, without turning round.*]

CATHLEEN: Did you see him riding down?

[MAURYA *goes on keening.*]

CATHLEEN [*A little impatiently.*]: God forgive you; isn't it a better thing to raise your voice and tell what you seen, than to be making lamentation for a thing that's done? Did you see Bartley, I'm saying to you.

MAURYA [*With a weak voice.*]: My heart's broken from this day.

CATHLEEN [*As before.*]: Did you see Bartley?

MAURYA: I seen the fearfulest thing.

CATHLEEN [*Leaves her wheel and looks out.*]: God forgive you; he's riding the mare now over the green head, and the gray pony behind him.

MAURYA [*Starts, so that her shawl falls back from her head and shows her white tossed hair. With a frightened voice.*]: The gray pony behind him.

CATHLEEN [*Coming to the fire.*]: What is it ails you, at all?

MAURYA [*Speaking very slowly.*]: I've seen the fearfulest thing any person has seen, since the day Bride Dara seen the dead man with a child in his arms.

CATHLEEN AND NORA: Uah.

[*They crouch down in front of the old woman at the fire.*]

NORA: Tell us what it is you seen.

MAURYA: I went down to the spring well, and I stood there saying a prayer to myself. Then Bartley came along, and he riding on the red mare with the gray pony behind him. [*She puts her hands, as if to hide something from her eyes.*] The Son of God spare us, Nora!

CATHLEEN: What is it you seen?

MAURYA: I seen Michael himself.

CATHLEEN [*Speaking softly.*]: You did not, Mother; it wasn't Michael you seen, for his body is after being found in the Far North, and he's got a clean burial by the grace of God.

MAURYA [*A little defiantly.*]: I'm after seeing him this day, and he riding and galloping. Bartley came first on the red mare; and I tried to say, "God speed you," but something choked the words in my throat. He went by quickly; and "The blessing of God on you," says he, and I could say nothing. I looked up then, and I crying, at the gray pony, and there was Michael upon it—with fine clothes on him, and new shoes on his feet.

CATHLEEN [*Begins to keen.*]: It's destroyed we are from this day. It's destroyed, surely.

NORA: Didn't the young priest say the Almighty God wouldn't leave her destitute with no son living?

MAURYA [*In a low voice, but clearly.*]: It's little the like of him knows of the sea. . . . Bartley will be lost now, and let you call in Eamon and make me a good coffin out of the white boards, for I won't live after them. I've had a husband, and a husband's father, and six sons in this house—six fine men, though it was a hard birth I had with every one of them and they coming to the world—and some of them were found and some of them were not found, but they're gone now the lot of them. . . . There were Stephen, and Shawn, were lost in the great wind, and found after in the Bay of Gregory of the Golden Mouth, and carried up the two of them on the one plank, and in by that door.

[She pauses for a moment, the girls start as if they heard something through the door that is half open behind them.]

NORA *[In a whisper.]*: Did you hear that, Cathleen? Did you hear a noise in the northeast?

CATHLEEN *[In a whisper.]*: There's some one after crying out by the seashore.

MAURYA *[Continues without hearing anything.]*: There was Sheamus and his father, and his own father again, were lost in a dark night, and not a stick or sign was seen of them when the sun went up. There was Patch after was drowned out of a curagh that turned over. I was sitting here with Bartley, and he a baby, lying on my two knees, and I seen two women, and three women, and four women coming in, and they crossing themselves, and not saying a word. I looked out then, and there were men coming after them, and they holding a thing in the half of a red sail, and water dripping out of it—it was a dry day, Nora—and leaving a track to the door.

[She pauses again with her hand stretched out toward the door. It opens softly and old women began to come in, crossing themselves on the threshold, and kneeling down in front of the stage with red petticoats over their heads.]

MAURYA *[Half in a dream, to* CATHLEEN.*]*: Is it Patch or Michael, or what is it at all?

CATHLEEN: Michael is after being found in the Far North, and when he is found there how could he be here in this place?

MAURYA: There does be a power of young men floating round in the sea, and what way would they know if it was Michael they had, or another man like him, for when a man is nine days in the sea, and the wind blowing, it's hard set his own mother would be to say what man was it.

CATHLEEN: It's Michael, God spare him, for they're after sending us a bit of his clothes from the Far North.

[She reaches out and hands MAURYA *the clothes that belonged to Michael.* MAURYA *stands up slowly, and takes them in her hands.* NORA *looks out.]*

NORA: They're carrying a thing among them and there's water dripping out of it and leaving a track by the big stones.

CATHLEEN *[In a whisper to the women who have come in.]*: Is it Bartley it is?

Interpretation

1. The mood of this cutting obviously is somber. How would you convey this feeling to an audience? How would you try to maintain it?

2. What provides the conflict? Where is the climax in this scene? What is the central idea?

3. How would you have the characters played to differentiate among them?

4. What sort of setting would you want to use? What sort of costumes? How would you block the cutting?

Act 3, scene 1

Blood Wedding

Federico García Lorca

This is a play of violent passion, a blending of lyricism and drama as well as of the human and the symbolic.

The action centers around two feuding families. The groom, who is the last living male in one of the families, courts a girl who has been involved with the only male of the other family who has not been imprisoned.

On the eve of her betrothal, the bride resumes relations with the other man, Leonardo, married and a father. The pair cannot control their passion; they love and hate each other at the same time. On the day of the wedding they run away together.

Pursued by the groom and his friends, they hide in a forest, where such allegorical characters as the Moon and Death appear.

Translated by Richard L. O'Connell

[*A forest. It is nighttime. Great moist tree trunks. A dark atmosphere. Two violins are heard. Three* WOODCUTTERS *enter.*]

FIRST WOODCUTTER: And have they found them?

SECOND WOODCUTTER: No. But they're looking for them everywhere.

THIRD WOODCUTTER: They'll find them.

SECOND WOODCUTTER: Sh-h-h!

THIRD WOODCUTTER: What?

SECOND WOODCUTTER: They seem to be coming closer on all the roads at once.

FIRST WOODCUTTER: When the moon comes out they'll see them.

SECOND WOODCUTTER: They ought to let them go.

FIRST WOODCUTTER: The world is wide. Everybody can live in it.

THIRD WOODCUTTER: But they'll kill them.

SECOND WOODCUTTER: You have to follow your passion. They did right to run away.

FIRST WOODCUTTER: They were deceiving themselves but at the last blood was stronger.

THIRD WOODCUTTER: Blood!

FIRST WOODCUTTER: You have to follow the path of your blood.

SECOND WOODCUTTER: But blood that sees the light of day is drunk up by the earth.

FIRST WOODCUTTER: What of it? Better dead with the blood drained away than alive with it rotting.

THIRD WOODCUTTER: Hush!

FIRST WOODCUTTER: What? Do you hear something?

THIRD WOODCUTTER: I hear the crickets, the frogs, the night's ambush.

FIRST WOODCUTTER: But not the horse.

THIRD WOODCUTTER: No.

FIRST WOODCUTTER: By now he must be loving her.

SECOND WOODCUTTER: Her body for him; his body for her.

THIRD WOODCUTTER: They'll find them and they'll kill them.

FIRST WOODCUTTER: But by then they'll have mingled their bloods. They'll be like two empty jars, like two dry arroyos.

SECOND WOODCUTTER: There are many clouds and it would be easy for the moon not to come out.

THIRD WOODCUTTER: The bridegroom will find them with or without the moon. I saw him set out. Like a raging star. His face the color of ashes. He looked the fate of all his clan.

FIRST WOODCUTTER: His clan of dead men lying in the middle of the street.

SECOND WOODCUTTER: There you have it!

THIRD WOODCUTTER: You think they'll be able to break through the circle?

SECOND WOODCUTTER: It's hard to. There are knives and guns for ten leagues 'round.

THIRD WOODCUTTER: He's riding a good horse.

SECOND WOODCUTTER: But he's carrying a woman.

FIRST WOODCUTTER: We're close by now.

SECOND WOODCUTTER: A tree with forty branches. We'll soon cut it down.

THIRD WOODCUTTER: The moon's coming out now. Let's hurry.

[*From the left shines a brightness.*]

FIRST WOODCUTTER: O rising moon!
Moon among the great leaves.

SECOND WOODCUTTER: Cover the blood with jasmines!

FIRST WOODCUTTER: O lonely moon!
Moon among the great leaves.

SECOND WOODCUTTER: Silver on the bride's face.

THIRD WOODCUTTER: O evil moon!
Leave for their love a branch in shadow.

FIRST WOODCUTTER: O sorrowing moon!
Leave for their love a branch in shadow.

Interpretation

1. What is the purpose of this scene?

2. Much of the language here is poetic. Why do you think García Lorca wrote it this way?

3. Is there conflict among the three woodcutters? Justify your answer.

4. What mood and atmosphere would you try to communicate to an audience with this cutting? How would you go about it? What emotions would you want to arouse in the viewer?

5. How do the three characters differ? Are there any distinguishing traits? If so, what are they? How would you individualize the characters for an audience?

CUTTINGS FOR Mixed Groups

Middle of the Night

Hamlet, Prince of Denmark

The Time of Your Life

Arms and the Man

The Time of Your Life
Photo courtesy of Kent State University Theatre, Kent, Ohio

Act 2, scene 3

Middle of the Night

Paddy Chayefsky

T his is the story of a middle-aged man and a young woman who
fall in love. Both of their families object to the idea and to their
wanting to marry. The Girl's family not only objects to the age
difference but to the fact that the Manufacturer's family is Jewish.
His family feels that at this stage of his life he should be settling into
the familiar, rather than subjecting himself to the Girl's style of
living.

   In this cutting, the Manufacturer's daughter is quizzing him about
the Girl. His sister, who lives with him, is also giving him a rough
time about the upcoming marriage.

THE DAUGHTER: You're going to get married, Pa?

THE MANUFACTURER: Well, I'll tell you the whole story.

THE DAUGHTER [*Fishing in her purse for cigarettes.*]: Do we know
   the woman, Pa?

THE MANUFACTURER: Well, you might. I don't know. She's a girl
   works up in my office. You probably saw her there. A blond
   girl. The receptionist, sits in front of Caroline.

   [THE SON-IN-LAW *again proffers his pack of cigarettes to his
   wife, who shakes her head and gets one out of her own.*]

THE SON-IN-LAW: Congratulations, Jerry.

THE MANUFACTURER: Thank you. I think you should know, she's
   quite a young girl. Twenty-four years old. She's younger than
   you are, Lillian. I've been seeing her for a couple of months,
   and it just seems that this is it.

   [*The brief enthusiasm of the previous moment seems to have
   filtered out. A short silence fills the room.* THE SISTER, *who had
   turned abruptly away at* THE MANUFACTURER'S *announcement,*

rubs her brow nervously with the tips of her fingers. THE SON-IN-LAW sends a cautious look to his wife and then looks back to the floor. THE DAUGHTER sits down again, takes a long puff on her cigarette. THE MANUFACTURER purses his lips.]

THE DAUGHTER [*Smiling briefly.*]: Well, that's wonderful, Pa. I'm very happy for you.

THE MANUFACTURER: Thank you, sweetheart, thank you. Nothing definite has been set. The girl has to get a divorce, she's in the process now. I'd like you to meet the girl. I'm sure you'll like her. We'll have to set up some kind of dinner. [*He considers the carpeting at his feet, takes a deep sigh.*] So that's it, that's my announcement.

THE SISTER [*Suddenly moves to her brother, bursting out.*]: Jerry, what are you doing? Do you know what you're doing? What's the matter with you?

THE MANUFACTURER: Evelyn, let me stop you before you even start.

THE SISTER: Honest to God, for God's sakes. All right, you come in, you tell me, a twenty-four-year-old girl. All right. What's the matter with you? You're a sensible man, for the love of God, honest to God. Our brother Herman, who is a fool—all right, this I could expect from him. But you're the sensible one. For God's sakes, what's the matter with you?

[THE MANUFACTURER *has moved a few steps toward his daughter.*]

THE MANUFACTURER [*To his daughter, with a vague smile.*]: I have to admit, Lillian, I expected a little more enthusiasm from you.

[THE DAUGHTER *looks up, smiles briefly.*]

THE DAUGHTER: I'm just a little shocked, Pa, to tell you the truth.

THE MANUFACTURER: It's really not such a shocking thing. I'm going to get married, that's all. Of course, she's a young girl, and this presents a number of problems, but . . .

THE SISTER [*To* THE SON-IN-LAW]: It never works out. I could tell you ten cases. When I had my apartment in Brooklyn, there was a man in the building, fifty-nine years old, he ran away with a sixteen-year-old girl. It was in the papers and everything. What a scandal. His wife had a nervous breakdown. [*Turns to her brother.*] Jerry, don't do something you'll regret the rest of your life. You're fifty-three years old. You're a man settled in habit. You like to come home, you watch television.

You want to get married, marry somebody your own age. Who is this girl? I want to know. Who is this girl? She sees a nice rich fellow, has a good business, makes a good living. She sees herself living in a fancy apartment, fancy clothes. . . .

THE MANUFACTURER: Evelyn, don't get so excited. You're beginning to say a lot of foolish things.

THE SISTER: Is she going to move in here?

THE MANUFACTURER: A married couple usually live together.

THE SISTER [*Throwing up her hands and moving away.*]: All right! You want to marry her, marry her. You want me to move out of the house? All right, I'll pack my clothes, I'll move out.

THE MANUFACTURER: Is that what's bothering you?

THE SISTER: What's bothering me is you're making a fool of yourself.

THE DAUGHTER: All right, Evelyn . . .

THE SISTER: You're making a fool of yourself, Jerry. I'm telling you right to your face. All right, you want to have an affair with a girl, all right. But marriage? Don't be a fool. It never works out. Max Coleman—you remember Max Coleman? I could tell you a hundred cases. Max Coleman married a girl of thirty-four, already a young woman, not a kid any more, and you saw what happened. One year, they were divorced. [THE MANUFACTURER *turns from his sister and moves slowly to his daughter.* THE SISTER *suddenly calls out.*] Is she Jewish?

THE MANUFACTURER [*Sitting down beside his daughter.*]: Does that matter in this day and age?

THE SISTER [*Paces nervously to another corner of the room, mutters.*]: All right, you want me to move out, I'll pack my clothes, I'll move out.

[THE MANUFACTURER *looks at his daughter.*]

THE MANUFACTURER: Lillian, I sense you're not entirely happy about the whole idea.

THE DAUGHTER: Pa, for heaven's sakes, you come in the room, you tell me you're going to get married to some girl. Give me a chance to digest it.

THE SISTER [*Calling out from her corner.*]: Do you remember Harry Wolfson? Used to live on Eastern Parkway when we used to live in Brooklyn. He also had a big romance with a young girl. A man gets to middle age, and he begins to worry about . . .

THE MANUFACTURER: What's so terrible about middle age? I'm physically in tiptop shape. Nat Phillips has been trying to get me interested in golf. Son of a gun, I'm going to take him up on it.

THE SISTER: Max Coleman married a girl of thirty-four, already a young woman, not a kid any more, and in one year . . .

THE MANUFACTURER: Max Coleman is an idiot, was an idiot, and always will be.

THE SISTER: Jerry, we went to Paul's New Year's Eve party last year. A bunch of young people, dancing and drinking. Didn't you tell me you felt out of place? For heaven's sakes, your own daughter Lillian is older than this girl. A young girl, twenty years old, what does she want? She wants night clubs, dancing. She's not going to sit with you, watch television every night. And don't say you're in such tiptop shape. You're not such an athlete any more. You've been complaining about your back for a good couple of years.

THE MANUFACTURER: Don't you think I considered all this? I'm a businessman, you know. I don't jump into propositions.

THE SISTER: Are you kidding yourself this girl's in love with you or something?

THE MANUFACTURER: Evelyn, this is really none of your goddam business.

THE SISTER: You said you wanted to discuss it.

THE MANUFACTURER [With sudden sharpness.]: I made an announcement! I didn't open the floor for discussions! I'm not a kid we're deciding to send to summer camp or not. I'm not a family problem.

THE SISTER [Throwing up her hands and turning away.]: All right! All right!

THE DAUGHTER: All right, Pa . . .

THE SISTER: You want me to pack my clothes, I'll move out, that's all.

THE DAUGHTER [Taking the older woman's arm.]: All right, Evelyn, don't get so upset.

[THE SISTER's eyes have become red.]

THE SISTER [*Shielding her eyes with a hand.*]: My whole life I gave up for my brothers and sisters. My whole life. Mama died, who brought up the family? My whole life I gave up.
[*She turns away from the others, moves quickly across the room.*]

THE MANUFACTURER: Nobody said you have to move out. Maybe we'll get a bigger apartment. I don't know. I haven't thought about it.

THE SISTER [*Shrilly.*]: I wouldn't live in the same house with that tramp!

THE MANUFACTURER [*Angrily.*]: All right! Shut up!

THE DAUGHTER: All right, Pa, all right.

THE MANUFACTURER: For God's sakes, the world isn't coming to an end. I'm just going to get married.

THE DAUGHTER [*Escorting him to a chair.*]: All right, Pa, don't get so angry.

[*A sudden, swift, inexplicable silence sweeps over the room, thick with the edges of unresolved angers.* THE MANUFACTURER *plucks at his trouser leg with nervous fingers.* THE DAUGHTER *sits down on the couch. Then, suddenly,* THE SISTER *whirls abruptly and goes sullenly up into the anteroom, disappearing into the apartment.* THE MANUFACTURER *looks up briefly, scowling at her departing back. He mutters to no one in particular, but really to his daughter.*]

THE MANUFACTURER: All she's worried about is she's going to have to move out of the house. She's the older sister, you know, so she feels everybody has to get her okay. That's why Herman never got married, do you know that? She wouldn't approve of any girl.

THE DAUGHTER: Pa, her position in your house is threatened, and she's fighting, that's all.

THE MANUFACTURER [*The anger flowing out of him.*]: This was not an easy decision for me. To get married, you know, at my age, and to a girl young enough to be my daughter . . . Don't you think I have doubts about what I'm doing? You know Walter Lockman tried to commit suicide yesterday?

THE DAUGHTER: No, I didn't know, Pa.

THE MANUFACTURER: Everybody gets to a certain age there, when suddenly old age with white hair, sitting in the park playing checkers . . . who wants to be an old fool? I'll tell you something. It's important to me that a young girl finds me attractive. I didn't know it was so important, but it's important. [*He leans to his daughter, a vague note of pleading slipping into his voice.*] She needs me, you understand, Lillian? It's been a long time since somebody needed me. My kids are all grown up, with children of their own. I'm a man who has to give of himself, I . . . [*He turns his face away and scowls. For a moment, nobody says anything. Then he stands, ostensibly looks for his jacket, which is draped over the back of the chair. He goes to it.*] I don't have to justify myself. I decided to get married, that's all.

THE DAUGHTER: Nobody said no, Pa.

THE MANUFACTURER [*Finding a cigar and taking it out.*]: She's a very sweet girl. Very bright, very clever. But emotionally, she's really immature. A neglected girl. She's so hungry for love. Like an orphan. She has to know twenty-four hours a day that you love her. [*Coming back to his daughter.*] All right, so who's perfect? Apparently, I'm attracted to childish women. Your mother, she should rest in peace, till the day she died she was fifteen years old. [*Sits down again, leans across to his daughter, the pleading naked on his face.*] But this girl is sweet, Lillian, I can't tell you. She has such delight in her. Like a baby. [*He looks at her, his eyes wide and beseeching.*] Do you think I'm making a fool of myself, Lillian?

THE DAUGHTER [*Drops her eyes, frowns.*]: Well, Pa, it's really not my business to interfere in your life.

THE MANUFACTURER: At least, a few years of happiness I'll have. Even a few years of happiness, you don't throw away.

THE DAUGHTER: I never met the girl, of course . . .
[THE DAUGHTER *scowls, looks away, then stands.*]

THE MANUFACTURER: Your opinion is very important to me, Lillian. I'll be honest with you. I'm not sure of myself in this thing. [THE DAUGHTER *is looking around for her cigarettes again.*] Don't go home yet, Lillian.

THE DAUGHTER: I'm just looking for my cigarettes, Pa. [*Her husband offers his pack; she takes one.*]

THE MANUFACTURER [*Rising and following her.*]: What I'm afraid, you see, is like Walter Lockman needs prostitutes maybe I need a young bride.

THE SON-IN-LAW [*Standing suddenly.*]: Jerry, you love her?

THE MANUFACTURER [*Turns to his* SON-IN-LAW]: Like a schoolboy.

THE SON-IN-LAW: And she loves you? So that's the whole thing. Get married.

THE DAUGHTER [*Snapping at her husband with rather sudden intensity.*]: Sit down and stay out of this. It's none of your business. [THE SON-IN-LAW, *stung a little, shuffles back to his chair.* THE DAUGHTER *turns to her father.*] Pa, I'm going to be frank with you. The relationship, to say the least, seems to be a neurotic one. The girl is obviously infantile in many ways. Otherwise, she wouldn't have to look to older men. I don't know the girl, but obviously she is very dependent, very infantile. And the whole relationship doesn't sound to me like the basis for a sound marriage. It sounds to me more like a father-daughter relationship than a husband-wife. It sounds like you want to adopt her, rather than marry her.

THE SON-IN-LAW [*Sitting in his chair, without looking up.*]: Your father's nobody's fool, Lilly.

THE DAUGHTER: Jack, please . . .

THE SON-IN-LAW: The man wants to get married. All he wants to know is that you're happy for him.

THE DAUGHTER: I don't want him to do something he'll regret the rest of his life. [*There is something familiar about the sentence she has just said that is unpleasant to* THE DAUGHTER *and makes her frown.*] I'm just saying, weigh the circumstances.

THE MANUFACTURER [*Stands but avoids the eyes of the others.*]: All right, all right. We discussed it enough. I don't want to talk about it any more. [*He puts the cigar down on an ash tray, crosses slowly to a window, looks out at the heavy snow.* THE SISTER *appears in the anteroom.*] I'd go out for a walk, except it's snowing so much. I can't stand snow. I wish I was going to Florida with you. I'd like to go to bed. I'm tired. I'm usually asleep by this hour. When you get to my age . . .
[*He breaks off, once more aware of his age.*]

THE DAUGHTER: Pa, all I'm trying to say is . . .

THE MANUFACTURER [*Crying out.*]: All right! I don't want to talk any more about it, do you hear me!
[*He starts up to the anteroom, but his sister's presence makes him turn, and instead he goes to the chair over which his jacket is draped, and takes it.*]

THE DAUGHTER: Pa, why don't you come home with Jack and me, don't go in to work tomorrow, spend a long week end at our house?

THE SISTER [*As her brother moves into the anteroom to go to the closet.*]: Jerry, where are you going? Go to bed, for God's sakes. What are you going down for, a paper, what?

THE MANUFACTURER [*Getting his coat out of the closet, mutters.*]: Look, leave me alone for a couple of minutes.

THE DAUGHTER [*Coming to him in the anteroom.*]: What did you say, Pa? I didn't hear what you said.

THE MANUFACTURER [*Turns to his daughter and cries out more in pain than in anger.*]: I said, "Leave me alone!"
[*Carrying his coat, he wrenches the door open and exits from the apartment. The door closes heavily behind him.* THE SISTER *lets out a deep sigh and comes down into the living room.*]

THE SISTER: All right, all right, it's not so bad, it's not so bad. He's all upset now. Tomorrow he'll be sulking. In a couple of days he'll be all right, same old Jerry. One thing I know, a man gets to middle age, God alone knows.

THE DAUGHTER [*Coming down into the living room to her husband, who is standing and glowering at the floor.*]: I knew something like this was going to happen. He lives here lonely. His friends have all died or moved to California. Naturally, he's going to . . .

THE SON-IN-LAW: Come on, let's go home.

THE DAUGHTER [*To her husband, who has walked to the anteroom.*]: Listen, Jack, I really don't think I can get away Monday for Florida. My father is going through a very crucial period now, and . . .

THE SON-IN-LAW [*Slowly bursting out with all the repressed submissiveness of years. He stares at his wife, the words stumbling out.*]: Boy, you're great! Boy, you're great! Sure, the trouble with Evelyn, she got a neurotic attachment! Holy Jesus Christ! He came to you, he says he's going to get married, and you whack him across the face with some two-bit psychology! Can't go to Florida now! I knew it! I knew it! Your father needs you! Oh, sure, boy! Your father needs you like a hole in the head! How many times I heard that? My father needs me! You need your father, that's what! I knew we weren't going to Florida! I knew it!

THE DAUGHTER: Jack . . .

THE SON-IN-LAW: You're the one! You! You! Who's all tied up with your father! Took me two years to get you to move to New Rochelle! Couldn't live half an hour away from your father!

THE DAUGHTER: Now, listen, Jack . . .

THE SON-IN-LAW: Shut up! I'm talking now! I'm going to Florida, you hear me?! I don't care whether you come! Everything is for your father! Three times a week you got to call him on the phone! I'm your husband, goddammit, you know that? Jesus Christ! How about me?! I want to go away for a vacation! How about thinking about me sometimes instead of your goddam father?!
[*The shrill, fierce, tortured fury is so new to him that he feels physically sick. He stands, hunches a little, his face forward, his mouth open as if he were retching, his breath coming in the deep, exhausted way of a truly ill man. Then he says quietly, his eyes closed.*] I'm sorry, Lillian, I'm sorry. Come on, let's go home.
[*He turns and shuffles to the front door, where he waits. His wife, who is standing, pained and shocked at the outburst, guilty, confused, shamed, now moves slowly to the steps of the living room.*]

THE DAUGHTER [*Looking at the floor as she goes.*]: I didn't know you felt so strongly about my father, Jack. [*She goes up into the anteroom.*] Would you like to have a cup of coffee before we start driving? [*Turning to her aunt.*] Evelyn, is there any coffee? [*She turns back to her husband.*] Jack . . .

THE SON-IN-LAW [*At the door, looking down.*]: Come on, let's go. It's late, and I got to drive the sitter home yet.
[THE SON-IN-LAW *disappears out into the landing.* THE DAUGHTER *frowns, pauses, turns to her aunt.*]

THE DAUGHTER: So, Evelyn, would you call me and let me know what happens?

THE SISTER: Listen, don't worry. You go home with Jack. He's tired and nervous.

THE DAUGHTER [*Nods nervously.*]: So good-bye. Call me if something happens.

THE SISTER: Nothing's going to happen.

THE DAUGHTER: All right, so call me.
[*She goes out, closing the door behind her.* THE SISTER *stands a moment, then turns to pick up the fruit bowl.*]

Interpretation

1. Who is the most important character in this scene? What makes you think so?

2. What constitutes the tension? The conflict?

3. Analyze each character. What are his or her dominant emotions?

4. What is the mood of the scene? What should an audience feel while viewing it?

5. What type of setting would you use? Why?

6. What can you tell about the relationships among the people? How do they feel about each other?

Act 3, scene 2

HAMLET, PRINCE of DENMARK

William Shakespeare

S worn to revenge by his father's ghost, Hamlet has tried to discover the extent of the conspiracy that has resulted in Claudius'
assumption of the throne. He is suspicious of Polonius, the lord
chamberlain, and does not even trust Polonius' daughter, Ophelia,
whom he formerly courted.

In this cutting Hamlet has devised a play that he is presenting to
try to force his uncle, the king, into admitting his guilt in the death
of Hamlet's father.

KING: How fares our cousin Hamlet?

HAMLET: Excellent, i' faith, of the chameleon's dish. I eat the air,
promise-crammed. You cannot feed capons so.[1]

KING: I have nothing with this answer,[2] Hamlet. These words are
not mine.

HAMLET: No, nor mine now.[3] [*To* POLONIUS.] My lord, you played
once i' the university, you say?

POLONIUS: That did I, my lord, and was accounted a good actor.

HAMLET: What did you enact?

[1]Excellent . . . so: Hamlet deliberately misunderstands and takes the question to mean, "What food are you eating?" The chameleon was believed to
feed on air. *Promise-crammed* means stuffed, like a capon or fatted chicken,
but with empty promises.
[2]I . . . answer: I cannot make sense of your answer
[3]nor . . . now: once words are spoken, they are no longer the property of the
speaker

POLONIUS: I did enact Julius Caesar. I was killed i' the Capitol. Brutus killed me.

HAMLET: It was a brute part of him to kill so capital a calf there. Be the players ready?

ROSENCRANTZ: Aye, my lord, they stay upon your patience.[4]

QUEEN: Come hither, my dear Hamlet, sit by me.

HAMLET: No, good Mother, here's metal more attractive.

POLONIUS [*To the* KING.]: Oh ho! Do you mark that?

HAMLET: Lady, shall I lie in your lap? [*Lying down at* OPHELIA'S *feet.*]

OPHELIA: No, my lord.

HAMLET: I mean, my head upon your lap?

OPHELIA: Aye, my lord.

HAMLET: Do you think I meant country matters?[5]

OPHELIA: I think nothing, my lord.

HAMLET: That's a fair thought to lie between maids' legs.

OPHELIA: What is, my lord?

HAMLET: Nothing.

OPHELIA: You are merry, my lord.

HAMLET: Who, I?

OPHELIA: Aye, my lord.

HAMLET: Oh God, your only jig-maker.[6] What should a man do but be merry? For look you how cheerfully my mother looks, and my father died within 's two hours.

OPHELIA: Nay, 'tis twice two months, my lord.

HAMLET: So long? Nay, then, let the Devil wear black, for I'll have a suit of sables.[7] Oh heavens! Die two months ago, and not forgotten yet? Then there's hope a great man's memory may outlive his life half a year. But, by 'r Lady, he must build churches then, or else shall he suffer not thinking on, with the

---

[4]stay . . . patience: wait for you to be ready
[5]country matters: refers to something indecent
[6]jig-maker: composer of jigs
[7]suit of sables: *sable* means black and also a sable gown, a trimmed robe worn by wealthy older gentlemen

hobbyhorse,[8] whose epitaph is "For, oh, for oh, the hobbyhorse is forgot."

[Hautboys[9] play. The dumb show enters.[10] Enter a KING *and a* QUEEN *very lovingly, the* QUEEN *embracing him and he her. She kneels, and makes show of protestation unto him. He takes her up, and declines his head upon her neck, lays him down upon a bank of flowers. She, seeing him asleep, leaves him. Anon comes in a fellow, takes off his crown, kisses it, and pours poison in the* KING's *ears, and exit. The* QUEEN *returns, finds the* KING *dead, and makes passionate action. The* POISONER, *with some two or three Mutes, comes in again, seeming to lament with her. The dead body is carried away. The* POISONER *woos the* QUEEN *with gifts. She seems loath and unwilling awhile, but in the end accepts his love. Exeunt.]*

OPHELIA: What means this, my lord?

HAMLET: Marry, this is miching mallecho.[11] It means mischief.

OPHELIA: Belike this show imports the argument[12] of the play.

[Enter PROLOGUE.*]*

HAMLET: We shall know by this fellow. The players cannot keep counsel, they'll tell all.

OPHELIA: Will he tell us what this show meant?

HAMLET: Aye, or any show that you'll show him. Be not you ashamed to show, he'll not shame to tell you what it means.

OPHELIA: You are naught,[13] you are naught. I'll mark the play.

PROLOGUE: For us, and for our tragedy,
Here stooping to your clemency,
We beg your hearing patiently.

HAMLET: Is this a prologue, or the posy of a ring?[14]

OPHELIA: 'Tis brief, my lord.

HAMLET: As woman's love.

---

[8]hobbyhorse: imitation horse worn by performers in a morris dance, disapproved of by the pious
[9]Hautboys: oboes
[10]dumb show enters: an artificial performance, something "stagy"
[11]miching mallecho: slinking mischief
[12]Argument: plot; she also is puzzled by the "dumb show"
[13]naught: disgusting
[14]posy . . . ring: It was the custom to inscribe rings with brief messages

[*Enter two* PLAYERS, KING *and* QUEEN.]

PLAYER KING: Full[15] thirty times hath Phoebus' cart[16] gone round
    Neptune's[17] salt wash and Tellus[18] orbèd ground,
    And thirty dozen moons with borrowed sheen[19]
    About the world have times twelve thirties been,
    Since love our hearts and Hymen[20] did our hands
    Unite commutual in most sacred bands.

PLAYER QUEEN: So many journeys may the sun and moon
    Make us again count o'er ere love be done!
    But, woe is me, you are so sick of late,
    So far from cheer and from your former state,
    That I distrust[21] you. Yet, though I distrust,
    Discomfort you, my lord, it nothing must.
    For women's fear and love holds quantity[22]
    In neither aught or in extremity.[23]
    Now what my love is, proof hath made you know,
    And as my love is sized, my fear is so.
    Where love is great, the littlest doubts are fear,
    Where little fears grow great, great love grows there.

PLAYER KING: Faith, I must leave thee,[24] love, and shortly too,
    My operant powers[25] their functions leave to do.
    And thou shalt live in this fair world behind,
    Honored, beloved, and haply one as kind
    For husband shalt thou—

PLAYER QUEEN: Oh, confound the rest!
    Such love must needs be treason in my breast.
    In second husband let me be accurst!
    None wed the second but who killed the first.

HAMLET [*Aside.*]: Wormwood,[26] wormwood.

PLAYER QUEEN: The instances[27] that second marriage move
    Are base respects of thrift,[28] but none of love.
    A second time I kill my husband dead
    When second husband kisses me in bed.

[15]Full . . . twain: the play is deliberately written in crude rhyming verse, full of ridiculous and bombastic phrases
[16]Phoebus' cart: the chariot of the sun   [17]Neptune: the sea god
[18]Tellus: the earth goddess
[19]borrowed sheen: light borrowed from the sun   [20]Hymen: god of marriage
[21]distrust: am anxious about   [22]quantity: a fixed or determined amount
[23]In . . . extremity: either nothing or too much   [24]leave thee: die
[25]operant powers: bodily strength   [26]Wormwood: bitterness
[27]instances: arguments   [28]Respects of thrift: consideration of gains

PLAYER KING: I do believe you think what now you speak,
But what we do determine oft we break.
Purpose is but the slave to memory,
Of violent birth but poor validity,
Which now, like fruit unripe, sticks on the tree
But fall unshaken when they mellow be.
Most necessary 'tis that we forget
To pay ourselves what to ourselves is debt.
What to ourselves in passion we propose,
The passion ending, doth the purpose lose.
The violence of either grief or joy
Their own enactures[29] with themselves destroy.
Where joy most revels, grief doth most lament,
Grief joys, joy grieves, on slender accident.
This world is not for aye,[30] nor 'tis not strange
That even our loves should with our fortunes change,
For 'tis a question left us yet to prove
Whether love lead fortune or else fortune love.
The great man down, you mark his favorite flies,
The poor advanced makes friends of enemies.
And hitherto doth love on fortune tend,
For who not needs shall never lack a friend,
And who in want a hollow friend doth try
Directly seasons[31] him his enemy.
But, orderly to end where I begun,
Our wills and fates do so contráry run
That our devices still are overthrown,
Our thoughts are ours, their ends none of our own.
So think thou wilt no second husband wed,
But die thy thoughts when thy first lord is dead.

PLAYER QUEEN: Nor earth to me give food nor Heaven light!
Sport and repose lock from me day and night!
To desperation turn my trust and hope!
An anchor's[32] cheer in prison be my scope!
Each opposite that blanks[33] the face of joy
Meet what I would have well and it destroy!
Both here and hence pursue me lasting strife
If, once a widow, ever I be wife!

HAMLET: If she should break it now!

---

[29]enactures: performances   [30]aye: ever   [31]seasons: ripens into
[32]anchor: hermit   [33]blanks: makes pale

PLAYER KING: 'Tis deeply sworn. Sweet, leave me here a while.
My spirits grow dull, and fain I would beguile
The tedious day with sleep. [Sleeps.]

PLAYER QUEEN: Sleep rock thy brain,
And never come mischance between us twain! [Exit.]

HAMLET: Madam, how like you this play?

QUEEN: The lady doth protest too much, methinks.

HAMLET: Oh, but she'll keep her word.

KING: Have you heard the argument?[34] Is there no offense in 't?

HAMLET: No, no, they do but jest, poison is jest—no offense i' the world.

KING: What do you call the play?

HAMLET: *The Mousetrap*.[35] Marry, how? Tropically.[34] This play is the image of a murder done in Vienna. Gonzago is the Duke's name, his wife, Baptista. You shall see anon. 'Tis a knavish piece of work, but what o' that? Your Majesty, and we that have free[37] souls, it touches us not. Let the galled[38] jade wince, our withers are unwrung.

[*Enter* LUCIANUS.] This is one Lucianus, nephew to the King.

OPHELIA: You are as good as a chorus,[39] my lord.

HAMLET: I could interpret between you and your love, if I could see the puppets dallying.[40]

OPHELIA: You are keen, my lord, you are keen.

HAMLET: It would cost you a groaning to take off my edge.

OPHELIA: Still better, and worse.

HAMLET: So you must take your husbands.[41] Begin, murderer. Pox, leave thy damnable faces and begin. Come, the croaking raven doth bellow for revenge.

[34]argument: plot
[35]Mousetrap: a device to entice a person to his or her own destruction
[36]Tropically: figuratively, with a pun on "trap"   [37]free: innocent
[38]galled . . . unwrung: let a horse with a sore back wince when saddled; our shoulders (being ungalled) do not have pain
[39]chorus: the chorus often introduced characters and talked about the play that was to follow
[40]puppets dallying: crude marionette shows and fairs. As they were put through their motions, the puppeteer explained what was happening.
[41]So . . . husbands: "for better or for worse"

LUCIANUS: Thoughts black, hands apt, drugs fit, and time
      agreeing,
   Confederate season, else no creature[42] seeing,
   Thou mixture rank of midnight weeds collected,
   With Hecate's ban[43] thrice blasted, thrice infected,
   Thy natural magic and dire property[44]
   On wholesome life usurp immediately.
   [*Pours the poison into the sleeper's ear.*]

HAMLET: He poisons him i' the garden for his estate.[45] His name's
   Gonzago. The story is extant, and written in very choice
   Italian. You shall see anon how the murderer gets the love of
   Gonzago's wife.

OPHELIA: The King rises.

HAMLET: What, frighted with false fire![46]

QUEEN: How fares my lord?

POLONIUS: Give o'er the play.

KING: Give me some light. Away!

POLONIUS: Lights, lights, lights!

[42]confederate . . . seeing: the time is ripe and there are no witnesses (to the
poisoning)   [43]Hecate's ban: the curse of the goddess of witchcraft
[44]property: nature   [45]estate: kingdom   [46]false fire: a mere show

Interpretation

1. What is the theme of the cutting? In your own words, trace and
describe the action.

2. What is the dominant mood?

3. What type of person is Hamlet?

4. Design a setting and block the action. Justify your choices.

5. What are the most important lines? The most important actions?
Why do you think so? How would you emphasize them?

6. What is Hamlet's motive or goal? What provides the conflict?

Act 1

The Time of Your Life

William Saroyan

The play, which takes place in Nick's waterfront saloon in San Francisco, has been called a "social fable." The saloon attracts a collection of outlandish customers. The characters are nonconformists who do not want to accept the values embraced by the larger part of society.

Although the characters are separate from life as it really is, the author does an excellent job of presenting several episodes concurrently.

HARRY [*As* NICK *returns.*]: You Nick?

NICK [*Very loudly.*]: *I am Nick.*

HARRY [*Acting.*]: Can you use a great comedian?

NICK [*Behind the bar.*]: Who, for instance?

HARRY [*Almost angry.*]: Me.

NICK: You? What's funny about you?

[DUDLEY *at the telephone, is dialing. Because of some defect in the apparatus the dialing is very loud.*]

DUDLEY: Hello. Sunset 7349? May I speak to Miss Elsie Mandelspiegel? [*Pause.*]

HARRY [*With spirit and noise, dancing.*]: I dance and do gags and stuff.

NICK: In costume? Or are you wearing your costume?

DUDLEY: All I need is a cigar.

KITTY [*Continuing the dream of grace.*]: I'd walk out of the house, and stand on the porch, and look at the trees, and smell the flowers, and run across the lawn, and lie down under a tree, and read a book. [*Pause.*] A book of poems, maybe.

DUDLEY [*Very, very clearly.*]: Elsie Mandelspiegel. [*Impatiently.*] She has a room on the fourth floor. She's a nurse at the Southern Pacific Hospital. Elsie Mandelspiegel. She works at night. Elsie. Yes. [*He begins waiting again.* WESLEY, *a colored boy, comes to the bar and stands near* HARRY, *waiting.*]

NICK: Beer?

WESLEY: No, sir. I'd like to talk to you.

NICK [*To* HARRY.]: All right. Get funny.

HARRY [*Getting funny, an altogether different person, an actor with great energy, both in power of voice, and in force and speed of physical gesture.*]: Now, I'm standing on the corner of Third and Market. I'm looking around. I'm figuring it out. There it is. Right in front of me. The whole city. The whole world. People going by. They're going somewhere. I don't know where, but they're going. I ain't going *anywhere*. Where the hell can you go? I'm figuring it out. All right, I'm a citizen. A fat guy bumps his stomach into the face of an old lady. They were in a hurry. Fat and old. *They bumped.* Boom. I don't know. It may mean war. *War.* Germany. England. Russia. I don't know for sure. [*Loudly, dramatically, he salutes, about faces, presents arms, aims, and fires.*] WAAAAAR. [*He blows a call to arms.* NICK *gets sick of this, indicates with a gesture that* HARRY *should hold it, and goes to* WESLEY.]

NICK: What's on your mind?

WESLEY [*Confused.*]: Well—

NICK: Come on. Speak up. Are you hungry, or what?

WESLEY: Honest to God, I ain't hungry. All I want is a job. I don't want no charity.

NICK: Well, what can you do, and how good are you?

WESLEY: I can run errands, clean up, wash dishes, anything.

DUDLEY [*On the telephone, very eagerly.*]: Elsie? Elsie, this is Dudley. Elsie, I'll jump in the bay if you don't marry me. Life isn't worth living without you. I can't sleep. I can't think of anything but you. All the time. Day and night and night and day. Elsie, I love you. I love you. What? [*Burning up.*] Is this

Sunset 7-3-4-9? [*Pause.*] 7943? [*Calmly, while* WILLIE *begins making a small racket.*] Well, what's your name? *Lorene?* Lorene Smith? I thought you were Elsie Mandelspiegel. What? Dudley. Yeah. Dudley R. Bostwick. Yeah. R. It stands for Raoul, but I never spell it out. I'm pleased to meet *you,* too. What? There's a lot of noise around here. [WILLIE *stops hitting the marble game.*] Where am I? At Nick's, on Pacific Street. I work at the S. P. I told them I was sick and they gave me the afternoon off. Wait a minute. I'll ask them. I'd like to meet *you,* too. Sure. I'll ask them. [*Turns around to* NICK.] What's this address?

NICK: Number 3 Pacific Street, you cad.

DUDLEY: Cad? You don't know how I've been suffering on account of Elsie. I take things too ceremoniously. I've got to be more lackadaisical. [*Into telephone.*] Hello, Elenore? I mean, Lorene. It's number 3 Pacific Street. Yeah. Sure. I'll wait for you. How'll you know me? You'll *know* me. I'll recognize *you.* Good-by, now. [*He hangs up.*]

HARRY [*Continuing his monologue, with gestures, movements, and so on.*]: I'm standing there. I didn't do anything to anybody. Why should I be a soldier? [*Sincerely, insanely.*] BOOOOOOOOOM. WAR! O.K. War. *I* retreat. *I* hate war. I move to Sacramento.

NICK [*Shouting.*]: All right, comedian. Lay off a minute.

HARRY [*Broken-hearted, going to* WILLIE.]: Nobody's got a sense of humor any more. The world's dying for comedy like never before, but nobody knows how to *laugh.*

NICK [*To* WESLEY.]: Do you belong to the union?

WESLEY: What union?

NICK: For the love of Mike, where've you been? Don't you know you can't come into a place and ask for a job and get one and go to work, just like that. You've got to belong to one of the unions.

WESLEY: I didn't know. I got to have a job. Real soon.

NICK: Well, you've got to belong to a union.

WESLEY: I don't want any favors. All I want is a chance to earn a living.

NICK: Go on into the kitchen and tell Sam to give you some lunch.

WESLEY: Honest, I ain't hungry.

DUDLEY [*Shouting.*]: What I've gone through for Elsie.

HARRY: I've got all kinds of funny ideas in my head to help make the world happy again.

NICK [*Holding* WESLEY.]: No, he isn't hungry.
[WESLEY *almost faints from hunger.* NICK *catches him just in time. The* ARAB *and* NICK *go off with* WESLEY *into the kitchen.*]

HARRY [*To* WILLIE.]: See if you think this is funny. It's my own idea. I created this dance myself. It comes after the monologue. [HARRY *begins to dance.* WILLIE *watches a moment, and then goes back to the game. It's a goofy dance, which* HARRY *does with great sorrow, but much energy.*]

Interpretation

1. There are three different stories with three different lines of conflict in this cutting. Trace each story line and decide how you would make the action easy to follow for the audience.

2. Determine the most important traits of Harry, Nick, Wesley, and Dudley.

3. What is the theme or central idea of this cutting?

4. Determine which characters are most important throughout the scene, and discuss how you would make each a point of focus when necessary.

5. What are the goals of each of the characters? What are the relationships among them?

6. Determine the blocking. Justify your decisions.

Act 2

Arms and the Man

George Bernard Shaw

S imilar to the characters in *The Time of Your Life,* those in this cutting are not really lifelike. Rather, they are exaggerated to point up the playwright's message that there is no romance involved in waging war.

In this cutting, Petkoff and Sergius reminisce about a Swiss soldier who defected. They do not know that the "young Bulgarian lady" who harbored the soldier was Raina.

RAINA [*Stooping and kissing her father.*]: Dear father! Welcome home!

PETKOFF [*Patting her cheek.*]: My little pet girl. [*He kisses her. She goes to the chair left by* NICOLA *for* SERGIUS, *and sits down.*]

CATHERINE: And so you're no longer a soldier, Sergius.

SERGIUS: I am no longer a soldier. Soldiering, my dear madam, is the coward's art of attacking mercilessly when you are strong, and keeping out of harm's way when you are weak. That is the whole secret of successful fighting. Get your enemy at a disadvantage; and never, on any account, fight him on equal terms.

PETKOFF: They wouldn't let us make a fair stand-up fight of it. However, I suppose soldiering has to be a trade like any other trade.

SERGIUS: Precisely. But I have no ambition to shine as a tradesman; so I have taken the advice of that bagman of a captain that settled the exchange of prisoners with us at Pirot, and given it up.

PETKOFF: What! that Swiss fellow? Sergius: I've often thought of that exchange since. He over-reached us about those horses.

SERGIUS: Of course he over-reached us. His father was a hotel and livery stable keeper; and he owed his first step to his knowledge of horse-dealing. [*With mock enthusiasm.*] Ah, he was a soldier: every inch a soldier! If only I had bought the horses for my regiment instead of foolishly leading it into danger, I should have been a field-marshal now!

CATHERINE: A Swiss? What was he doing in the Serbian army?

PETKOFF: A volunteer, of course; keen on picking up his profession. [*Chuckling.*] We shouldn't have been able to begin fighting if these foreigners hadn't shewn us how to do it: we knew nothing about it; and neither did the Serbs. Egad, there'd have been no war without them!

RAINA: Are there many Swiss officers in the Serbian Army?

PETKOFF: No. All Austrians, just as our officers were all Russians. This was the only Swiss I came across. I'll never trust a Swiss again. He humbugged us into giving him fifty ablebodied men for two hundred worn out chargers. They weren't even eatable!

SERGIUS: We were two children in the hands of that consummate soldier, Major: simply two innocent little children.

RAINA: What was he like?

CATHERINE: Oh, Raina, what a silly question!

SERGIUS: He was like a commercial traveller in uniform. Bourgeois to his boots!

PETKOFF [*Grinning.*]: Sergius: tell Catherine that queer story his friend told us about how he escaped after Slivnitza. You remember. About his being hid by two women.

SERGIUS [*With bitter irony.*]: Oh yes: quite a romance! He was serving in the very battery I so unprofessionally charged. Being a thorough soldier, he ran away like the rest of them, with our cavalry at his heels. To escape their sabres he climbed a waterpipe and made his way into the bedroom of a young Bulgarian lady. The young lady was enchanted by his persuasive commercial traveller's manners. She very modestly entertained him for an hour or so, and then called in her mother lest her conduct should appear unmaidenly. The old lady was equally fascinated; and the fugitive was sent on his way in the morning, disguised in an old coat belonging to the master of the house, who was away at the war.

RAINA [*Rising with marked stateliness.*]: Your life in the camp has made you coarse, Sergius. I did not think you would have repeated such a story before me. [*She turns away coldly.*]

CATHERINE [*Also rising.*]: She is right, Sergius. If such women exist, we should be spared the knowledge of them.

PETKOFF: Pooh! nonsense! what does it matter?

SERGIUS [*Ashamed.*]: No, Petkoff: I was wrong. [*To* RAINA *with earnest humility.*]: I beg your pardon. I have behaved abominably. Forgive me, Raina. [*She bows reservedly.*] And you too, madam. [CATHERINE *bows graciously and sits down. He proceeds solemnly, again addressing* RAINA.] The glimpses I have had of the seamy side of life during the last few months have made me cynical; but I should not have brought my cynicism here: least of all into your presence. Raina. I—[*Here, turning to the others, he is evidently going to begin a long speech when the Major interrupts him.*]

PETKOFF: Stuff and nonsense, Sergius! That's quite enough fuss about nothing: a soldier's daughter should be able to stand up without flinching to a little strong conversation. [*He rises.*] Come: it's time for us to get to business. We have to make up our minds how those three regiments are to get back to Philippopolis: there's no forage for them on the Sofia route. [*He goes towards the house.*] Come along. [SERGIUS *is about to follow him when* CATHERINE *rises and intervenes.*]

CATHERINE: Oh, Paul, can't you spare Sergius for a few moments? Raina has hardly seen him yet. Perhaps I can help you to settle about the regiments.

SERGIUS [*Protesting.*]: My dear madam, impossible: you—

CATHERINE [*Stopping him playfully.*]: You stay here, my dear Sergius: there's no hurry. I have a word or two to say to Paul. [SERGIUS *instantly bows and steps back.*] Now, dear [*Taking* PETKOFF'S *arm.*]: come and see the electric bell.

PETKOFF: Oh, very well, very well.

Interpretation

1. Analyze and discuss each of the characters.

2. Raina and Catherine are the women who hid the soldier. Why do they react as they do to the story about this? What emotions do you think each feels?

3. As a director, how would you try to convey the comedy of this cutting?

4. What provides the conflict in this scene?

NTC LANGUAGE ARTS BOOKS

Business Communication
Business Communication Today!
 Thomas & Fryar
Handbook for Business Writing,
 Baugh, Fryar & Thomas

Essential Skills
The Book of Forms for Everyday
 Living, *Rogers*
Building Real Life English Skills,
 Starkey & Penn
English Survival Series, *Maggs*
Essential Life Skills Series
Everyday Consumer English,
 Kleinman & Weissman

Genre Literature
Another Tomorrow: A Science Fiction
 Anthology, *Hollister*
The Detective Story, *Schwartz*
The Short Story & You, *Simmons &
 Stern*
You and Science Fiction, *Hollister*

Journalism
Getting Started in Journalism,
 Harkrider
Journalism Today! *Ferguson & Patten*

Language, Writing and Composition
An Anthology for Young Writers,
 Meredith
The Art of Composition, *Meredith*
Lively Writing, *Schrank*
Look, Think & Write, *Leavitt & Sohn*
Writing in Action, *Meredith*
Writing by Doing, *Sohn & Enger*

Media
Photography in Focus, *Jacobs &
 Kokrda*
Television Production Today! *Kirkham*
Understanding Mass Media, *Schrank*
Understanding the Film, *Johnson &
 Bone*

Mythology
Mythology and You, *Rosenberg &
 Baker*
Welcome to Ancient Greece, *Millard*
Welcome to Ancient Rome, *Millard*
World Mythology, *Rosenberg*

Reading
Reading by Doing, *Simmons & Palmer*

Speech
The Basics of Speech, *Galvin, Cooper
 & Gordon*
Contemporary Speech, *HopKins &
 Whitaker*
Creative Speaking, *Buys, et al.*
Creative Speaking Series
Dynamics of Speech, *Myers &
 Herndon*
Getting Started in Public Speaking,
 Prentice & Payne
Listening by Doing, *Galvin*
Literature Alive! *Gamble & Gamble*
Person to Person, *Galvin & Book*
Public Speaking Today! *Prentice &
 Payne*
Speaking by Doing, *Buys, Sills & Beck*

Theatre
The Book of Cuttings for Acting &
 Directing, *Cassady*
The Book of Scenes for Acting
 Practice, *Cassady*
The Dynamics of Acting, *Snyder &
 Drumsta*
An Introduction to Theatre and Drama,
 Cassady & Cassady
Play Production Today! *Beck, et al.*

For a current catalog and information about our complete line
of language arts books, write:
National Textbook Company,
a division of NTC Publishing Group
4255 West Touhy Avenue
Lincolnwood (Chicago), Illinois 60646-1975 U.S.A.